EMPLOYEE-CENTERED MANAGEMENT

A Strategy for High Commitment and Involvement

Frederick E. Schuster

Quorum Books   Westport, Connecticut
London

Library of Congress Cataloging-in-Publication Data

Schuster, Fred E.
    Employee-centered management : a strategy for high commitment and
involvement / Frederick E. Schuster.
        p. cm.
    Includes bibliographical references and index.
    ISBN 1-56720-187-3 (alk. paper)
    1. Industrial managment. I. Title.
HD31.S341563   1998
658.3—dc21   97-41003

British Library Cataloguing in Publication Data is available.

Library of Congress Catalog Card Number: 97-41003
ISBN: 1-56720-187-3

First published in 1998

Quorum Books, 88 Post Road West, Westport, CT 06881
An imprint of Greenwood Publishing Group, Inc.

Printed in the United States of America

The paper used in this book complies with the
Permanent Paper Standard issued by the National
Information Standards Organization (Z39.48-1984).

10 9 8 7 6 5 4 3 2 1

To Elizabeth, Fritz, Hilary, Joseph, and Emily—
my family, my life

CONTENTS

Part II: Implementing Strategy A

ILLUSTRATIONS

PREFACE

Do you want your employees to be more productive? Pay more attention to them! A significant relationship exists between attention to employees and superior organizational performance. This is the conclusion of numerous research studies, including one that focused on the management practices of 1300 major firms in America. These studies show a clear relationship between the practices used in managing employees and profitability.

This book documents a proven strategy for implementing change in an organization's culture to promote employee commitment, innovation, productivity, excellence, and success. But these data are only a part of the picture; conclusions, like theories, must be implemented in order to have practical value. Consequently, the greater part of this book presents an explanation of how the findings can be applied, as well as prescriptions for translating these findings into measurable improvements in organizational performance.

The prescriptions follow a seven-step process called Strategy A. Strategy A is designed to serve the needs of executives who wish to lead their organizations in a transition from a traditional bureaucratic culture to a high-involvement, motivational culture as emphasized by such organizations as Motorola, Hewlett-Packard, and Walt Disney. Strategy A is a framework for such a transition that provides practical step-by-step guidance on where to begin and how to proceed. This book is written for executives and managers, and aspiring executives and managers, in all types of organizations.

The first part of the book is a general outline of the strategy, its origins, and some discussion of firms that have inspired and/or implemented its use. The second part outlines specific steps to bring about culture change through Strategy A, and gives specific examples of companies using it.

Over the past few years, a great deal of publicity has been given to Japanese firms, both in Japan and in America, that have used an employee-centered style of management to achieve levels of productivity and quality that far excel those of their American competitors. The Japanese deserve a great deal of credit for so eagerly putting these theories into practice, but the idea of participative management actually had its origins in the United States. Unfortunately it has not been as widely applied in this country as in Japan.

Survival of the fittest dictates that many more organizations in America will move toward the employee-centered style of management. Companies that begin to pay more attention to employees will forge ahead, while others will fail to remain competitive.

Because of competition, the topic of organizational culture has received unparalleled attention in recent years. It has become apparent that "shared values" affect performance and morale in numerous ways; as a result, there is a critical need to understand how to manage culture. In short, how can an organization's culture be assessed and, if found dysfunctional, changed to a more adaptive one?

Strategy A is not a quick-fix approach to changing organization culture or a gimmick. It is a practical strategy solidly based on empirical research involving the best management practices of 1300 major firms. It is a strategy for bringing about a fundamental, bone-deep change in an organization's culture.

Strategy A emphasizes attention to the needs of employees as a key means for achieving high productivity. Its objective is to lay out an easy-to-follow, step-by-step strategy for changing an organization culture to achieve higher performance.

Strategy A is a structured process to move organizations away from management by direction and control (Theory X) and toward management by commitment and self-control (Theory Y). Commitment and self-control is inherently a more efficient form of management because it reduces the need for a whole layer of middle management, and simultaneously energizes front-line employees who produce the organization's product or provide its service. It is the way in which the most successful organizations in America are already managed, and it is where other organizations must move if they wish to remain (or become) competitive.

I would like to thank several people for their significant contributions to this book: Christine Hagan, doctoral candidate at Florida Atlantic University, for her contribution to the literature survey in Chapters 1 and 2; Larry Morden, of Ault Foods, Ltd.; and Tom Baker and Ian McKay of People Interactions Inc., for their contributions to Chapter 5; and Karen Dunning of Motorola Corporation for her contribution to the data analysis and graph in Chapter 5. I would like to thank each of the people just named also for their permission to include in the Appendix a research article we jointly authored. This article provides details of the research design and analysis that will be of interest to some readers.

Finally, I would like to especially thank my wife, Elizabeth, for her invaluable assistance and advice at every stage of this project.

Part I:
The Genesis of Strategy A

1 WHY WORRY ABOUT ORGANIZATION CULTURE?

A 1986 study of the 1000 largest industrial and 300 largest non-industrial firms in the United States found a significant relationship between employee-centered management practices and the financial performance of firms. Numerous later studies have now solidly documented the potential of employee involvement in achieving superior organizational performance.

These studies consistently point to the conclusion that a key to organizational effectiveness is broadly skilled, knowledgeable workers who are empowered and highly motivated. For organizations to be maximally effective over the long term, traditional hierarchies must be transformed into organizations in which individuals know more, do more, and contribute more. This high-involvement or employee-centered management model is based on the belief that people can be trusted to make important decisions about the management of their work. This approach puts knowledge, power, rewards, and a communications network in place at every level in an organization. It encourages employees to know how to do their work, to care about it, and to do it as well as it can possibly be done. These studies uniformly conclude that an indispensable ingredient for sustained competitive advantage is a management system that creates and maintains a high-involvement, employee-centered environment.

Nevertheless, despite the mounting evidence of superior financial performance by high-involvement organizations and the widely publicized outstanding performance of such firms as Hewlett-Packard, Southwest Airlines, and Walt Disney, employee-centered management is still not widely practiced in the United States. Although its use is slowly increasing, it is perhaps surprising, given its track record, that employee-centered management has not become the latest "fad." It seems reasonable to ask, "Why has American management been so reluctant, at least so slow, to adopt employee-centered management, when improved performance is being so eagerly sought by many organizations?" The reasons appear to be multiple and complex:

1. Complacency and inertia. *Until recently,* many executives never questioned or considered changing the status quo, which seemed fairly comfortable.
2. Short time-span focus of management systems in general, and reward systems in particular. Performance bonuses and other executive incentive plans are often tied to performance in one year, rather than to building a committed workforce (which is a long-term task).
3. Lack of *measurement* of human resource management practices. Until recently, little attention has been paid to executive performance regarding effective utilization of human resources, in part because standards for comparison did not exist. Our lack of *control* over the efficient utilization of the most expensive single cost of operation in many organizations is indeed remarkable.
4. Management's reluctance to give up special status, privileges, and power.
5. The fact that many managers have now become convinced that they would genuinely like to implement employee-centered management, but are unsure how to begin or exactly how to proceed—perhaps the most significant explanation.

As a result, innovation in management has not kept pace with changes in technology or products. Managements that take pride in being at the leading edge in developing new products or manufacturing technology are hopelessly mired in management practices that have changed little since the 1930s. What is needed is commitment to a concrete strategy for improving organization performance through employee-centered management.

DOES YOUR ORGANIZATION HAVE A HIGH-PERFORMANCE CULTURE?

Organizations that want their employees to be more productive should pay more attention to them. Research studies demonstrate conclusively that a significant relationship exists between employee-centered management and superior organizational performance. Over the last several years, a great deal of publicity has also been given to Japanese firms that have used an employee-centered style of management to achieve levels of quality that exceed their American competitors. While the Japanese deserve a great deal of credit for demonstrating the potency of high-involvement management, it was actually invented in America. Unfortunately, however, despite some progress, it is still not as widely applied in America as in Japan.

Survival of the fittest dictates that many more organizations in America will move toward the employee-centered style of management. Companies that begin to pay more attention to employees will forge ahead, while others fail to remain competitive. Organizations need to learn how to manage their culture.

If you would like to evaluate the impact on performance of your organization's culture, begin by answering the 20 questions in the following questionnaire as objectively as you can:

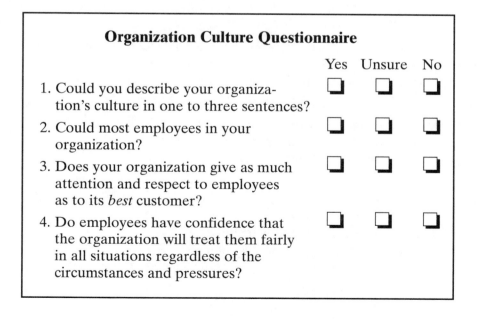

Organization Culture Questionnaire

	Yes	Unsure	No
1. Could you describe your organization's culture in one to three sentences?	❏	❏	❏
2. Could most employees in your organization?	❏	❏	❏
3. Does your organization give as much attention and respect to employees as to its *best* customer?	❏	❏	❏
4. Do employees have confidence that the organization will treat them fairly in all situations regardless of the circumstances and pressures?	❏	❏	❏

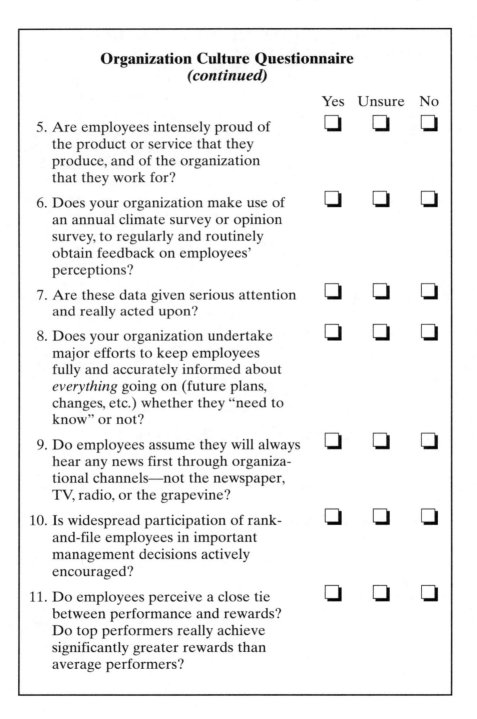

Organization Culture Questionnaire
(continued)

	Yes	Unsure	No
5. Are employees intensely proud of the product or service that they produce, and of the organization that they work for?	❑	❑	❑
6. Does your organization make use of an annual climate survey or opinion survey, to regularly and routinely obtain feedback on employees' perceptions?	❑	❑	❑
7. Are these data given serious attention and really acted upon?	❑	❑	❑
8. Does your organization undertake major efforts to keep employees fully and accurately informed about *everything* going on (future plans, changes, etc.) whether they "need to know" or not?	❑	❑	❑
9. Do employees assume they will always hear any news first through organizational channels—not the newspaper, TV, radio, or the grapevine?	❑	❑	❑
10. Is widespread participation of rank-and-file employees in important management decisions actively encouraged?	❑	❑	❑
11. Do employees perceive a close tie between performance and rewards? Do top performers really achieve significantly greater rewards than average performers?	❑	❑	❑

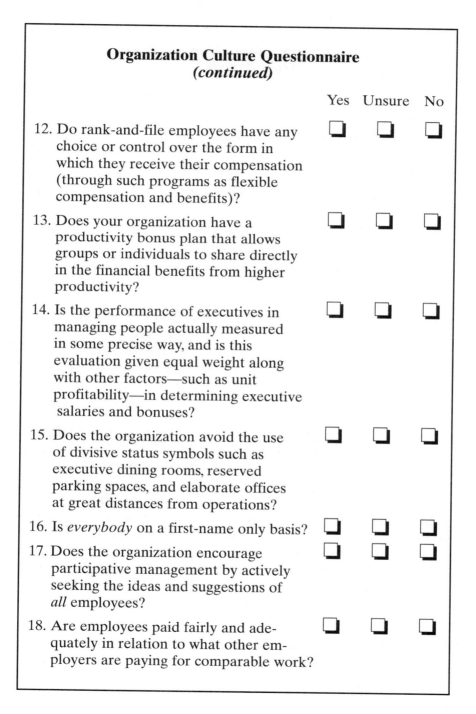

Organization Culture Questionnaire
(continued)

	Yes	Unsure	No
12. Do rank-and-file employees have any choice or control over the form in which they receive their compensation (through such programs as flexible compensation and benefits)?	❏	❏	❏
13. Does your organization have a productivity bonus plan that allows groups or individuals to share directly in the financial benefits from higher productivity?	❏	❏	❏
14. Is the performance of executives in managing people actually measured in some precise way, and is this evaluation given equal weight along with other factors—such as unit profitability—in determining executive salaries and bonuses?	❏	❏	❏
15. Does the organization avoid the use of divisive status symbols such as executive dining rooms, reserved parking spaces, and elaborate offices at great distances from operations?	❏	❏	❏
16. Is *everybody* on a first-name only basis?	❏	❏	❏
17. Does the organization encourage participative management by actively seeking the ideas and suggestions of *all* employees?	❏	❏	❏
18. Are employees paid fairly and adequately in relation to what other employers are paying for comparable work?	❏	❏	❏

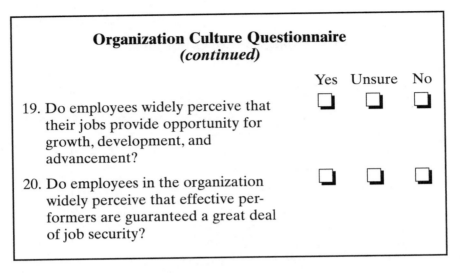

Score Your Organization's Culture

Count the total number of times you answered "yes" in the questionnaire. Ignore any answers of either "no" or "unsure."

A score of 16 or more means that your organization already has a high-performance culture. Other aspects of strategy (product, technology, marketing, and so forth) are of course also important, but your organization culture should provide a strong base for implementing strategy.

A score of 11 to 15 means that your organization probably has opportunities for improving organization culture. Increased attention to managing culture should enable the organization to achieve higher performance.

A score of ten or less means that your organization is clearly falling short of using culture for maximum competitive advantage. At *best*, culture may be a nonfactor in accomplishing organization strategy; more likely, it is a hindrance or a block.

If your organization scored 15 or less in this analysis, it would probably benefit from a program of planned change moving the organization toward employee-centered management.

ORGANIZATION CULTURE AND BOTTOM-LINE RESULTS

A more technical description of the research described here may be found in F. E. Schuster, D. L. Morden, T. E. Baker, I. S. McKay,

K. E. Dunning, and C. M. Hagan, "Management practice, organization climate, and performance: An exploratory study," *Journal of Applied Behavioral Science* (June 1997). This article is reprinted in the Appendix of this book for those readers who are interested in the technical details of the research.

An earlier study—F. E. Schuster, *The Schuster report: The proven connection between people and profits* (New York: John Wiley & Sons, 1986)—of the 1000 largest industrial and 300 largest nonindustrial firms in the United States found a significant relationship between employee-centered management and the financial performance of firms. In this study *employee-centered management* was defined as a strategy for achieving high levels of employee motivation, commitment, and performance through management practices (such as participation and involvement) that emphasize attention to employee needs and goals.

Other studies—R. Blackburn and B. Rosen, "Total quality and human resources management: Lessons learned from Baldrige award-winning companies," *Academy of Management Executive* 7(3), 1993: 49–66; E. E. Lawler III, *High involvement management: Participative strategies for improving organizational performance* (San Francisco: Jossey Bass, 1986); E. E. Lawler III, *The ultimate advantage: Creating the high involvement organization* (San Francisco: Jossey Bass, 1992)—have strongly supported the role of employee involvement in achieving improved organizational performance.

Employee involvement has been defined by Lawler as consisting of four critical organizational processes: information sharing, training, decision making, and rewards. According to Lawler, employee involvement refers to the degree to which these four key processes are moved down to the lowest levels in the organization.

Lawler contends that the key to organizational effectiveness lies in completely changing the way organizations are managed. In order to be competitive, organizations will require highly skilled, knowledgeable workers and a relatively stable workforce. Traditional hierarchies must be transformed into organizations in which individuals know more, do more, and contribute more. This high-involvement or employee-centered management model is based on the belief that people can be trusted to make important decisions about the management of their work. This approach puts knowledge, power, rewards, and a communications network in place at every level in an organization. It encourages employees to know how to do their work, to care about it, and to do it as well as it can possibly be done.

It is important to note, according to Lawler, that the real basis for competitive advantage lies in the management systems that create and sustain this environment. He cautions us not to confuse effective management systems with high-quality employees:

This is a mistake—the two are quite different. . . . Having high-quality employees does not assure an organization of having sustainable competitive advantage or even a short-term advantage. If the employees are poorly motivated or if the correct organization systems are not in place, the employees' talent may be wasted.

According to Lawler, an organization becomes employee-centered through a carefully managed process that strives for participation to integrate the individual with the organization in order to achieve high productivity and competitive advantage. This process involves restructuring the work so that it is as challenging, interesting, and motivating as possible. Individuals at all levels are given power to influence decisions; they are given information about the organization's operations and performance; they are trained so that they can operate with a good understanding of the business.

If the smoothly-running assembly line is the best image for the control-oriented approach, then the small business unit that controls its own fate and involves everyone in the business is the best image for the involvement-oriented approach.

M. A. Huselid, in "The impact of human resources management practices on turnover, productivity, and corporate financial performance," *Academy of Management Journal* 38(3), 1995: 635–672, has recently reported similar results in a parallel study.

Only in the past few years have empirical studies begun to quantitatively measure organization climate and its relationship to organization performance. For example, Kotter and Heskett (J. P. Kotter and J. L. Heskett, *Corporate culture and performance.* New York: Free Press, 1992) studied the relationship between culture and long-term economic performance across more than 200 organizations and conclude that:

1. Corporate culture can have a significant impact on a firm's long-term economic performance.
2. Corporate culture will probably be an even more important factor in determining the success or failure of firms in the next decade.

3. Corporate cultures that inhibit strong financial performance are not rare; they develop easily, even in firms that are full of reasonable and intelligent people.
4. Although tough to change, corporate cultures can be made more performance enhancing.

In a very influential book (J. Pfeffer, *Competitive advantage through people*. Boston: Harvard Business School Press, 1994), and in an article in the 25th Anniversary Issue of *Organizational Dynamics* (J. Pfeffer, "When it comes to best practices—why do smart organizations occasionally do dumb things?" *Organizational Dynamics*, Summer 1996, pp. 33–44), Jeffrey Pfeffer makes a powerful statement about the potential of the effective management of people for producing sustainable competitive advantage. He goes on to observe, however, that the practices he recommends have not yet been widely adopted, and ends the article with the admonition that implementation will not be easy regardless of how sensible the practices may be. He suggests four reasons for this: strategy and financial barriers, social barriers, power and political barriers, and hierarchical barriers. Schuster (1986) has also suggested a fifth barrier—the lack of a concrete strategy to give direction and support to such a transition.

The central proposition that emerges from all of these studies is that conscious interventions to move an organization toward emphasizing high levels of employee involvement and enhanced emphasis on meeting employee needs can produce higher motivation and commitment, which lead to improved organizational performance.

WHAT IS ORGANIZATION CULTURE AND WHY IS IT IMPORTANT?

Since this whole book is about changing organization cultures, let's start by discussing what organization culture is and why it is important. Organization culture is the system of beliefs, attitudes, values, and norms that are shared by members of an organization and that determine the characteristic pattern of behavior in relation to customers, product or service, other people within the organization, and the goals of the organization. There are three primary components of culture:

- the organization's history and traditions (who founded us; why; and under what conditions)

- the current operations (who we are; what we do; what we stand for; what our standards, values, ideals, and goals are)
- our vision for the future

These three components of culture can be translated simply as the organization's past, present, and future.

Put succinctly, organization culture is the most important single element of organizational strategy. In terms of its impact on organization success, it is more important than product, more important than markets, and more important than technical skills and unique competence.

Perhaps the easiest way to explain *why* culture is so important is to cite a personal experience. A few years ago I made a last-minute trip from my home in Florida to a city in the Northeast. Because the trip was not planned in advance, I traveled to my destination on an airline I don't usually fly. After we boarded the flight, the takeoff was delayed about 30 minutes because of bad weather at our destination.

I happened to be seated next to the galley, and the whole time we were waiting on the ground the cabin personnel (instead of going around the cabin trying to make passengers comfortable) stood there and complained about the airline. They complained about the crew scheduling, which they said was unfair. They complained about the company attitude of not caring about employees. They ran down their supervisor and the entire management of the airline. They moaned about a current pay dispute. In short, they spent the time of the delay criticizing every aspect of the organization.

After about 20 minutes of this diatribe, two thoughts popped into my mind:

- I wonder if the pilot feels the same way.
- I'll never ride this airline again if I can help it.

An ironic footnote is that this airline was currently spending millions of dollars each year putting its president on television to tell the public about the airline's dedication to excellent customer service. But who was I going to believe, the president on television, or the two crew members standing in front of me?

The sequel to this story is that the following day, when my business was completed, I returned home on a different airline. When I got on, the cabin attendant greeted me with a smile, took my briefcase and coat to put in the rack for me, and asked if she could bring me a drink. Because it was raining hard, I asked if she knew whether we would leave on time. Her reply was, "We'll do our very best, sir; that's the Delta way." What's more, I think she really meant it.

So let me ask you, which airline do you think I will do everything possible to take next time? Assuming these two incidents go on hundreds of times each day (and I'm fairly sure they do, because a lot of other travelers seem to share my opinions about the two carriers), which of these airlines has the better public image? To which of these airlines do you suppose the employees contributed their own money to buy a plane for the company as a token of appreciation for the way they have been treated? Which of these airlines do you suppose is still growing and prospering? And which one do you suppose is now bankrupt and out of business?

Keep in mind that the planes these two companies flew were essentially identical; their schedules were similar; and the *technical* products were essentially identical. The only things really different about these two companies are the service aspect of their transactions with the public and the attitude—and both of those outcomes are products of the organization culture.

So culture is everything! It is literally the most important determinant of the success and future viability of these two organizations—and yours. Incidentally, every organization does have a culture—whether it is sharply focused or only vaguely perceived; whether it supports high performance, or blocks it.

2 THE ORIGINS OF STRATEGY A

In the early 1990s, a number of forces in the business environment of the United States called unprecedented attention to the importance of the human organization and demonstrated to executives that human resources hold the key to the competitiveness of the U.S. economy. These forces included greatly increased foreign competition in many traditional U.S. markets, persistent slow growth in productivity, and significant changes in the American workforce. Although they were interrelated and tended to reinforce one another, to some extent these forces were also independent. Furthermore, they will continue to impact organizations for the next twenty years. The logical point at which to begin this discussion, then, is to examine some of these pressures.

WHY PRODUCTIVITY IS IMPORTANT

The stagnation of productivity growth has been a continuing concern for several years. Much of the industrial success of the United States and much of its managerial philosophy has been built on the assumption that productivity will always continue to increase. This had, in fact, been the case from the onset of industrialization in the United States up to the 1960s.

A serious slippage in the rate of increase in hourly productivity first began in the mid-1960s, when the rate of increase dropped to around 3 percent per year. Although this was lower than the historical average (6 percent) in the United States, and far lower than that in competing nations such as Japan and Germany, the figure was at first viewed as merely a temporary problem that needed to be solved.

Toward the end of the 1960s, however, the rate of increase slowed even further, and in the 1970s, it was close to zero. Productivity improved slightly in the 1980s, but generally trailed productivity growth in Japan and Germany. As a result, the United States found itself less and less able to compete in many of its traditional markets. Although productivity growth in the United States has improved slightly in the 1990s (particularly in 1996 and 1997), it is still nowhere near our historical average. As a result, significant increases in productivity remain a critical strategic goal of most domestic firms, where significant increases in productivity would translate into substantial competitive advantage.

It must be understood, however, that productivity is not easy to measure accurately, particularly in the case of service and knowledge workers such as teachers, symphony conductors, and police, or those involved in research and development. Although the output of these occupations can be assessed with some gross volume measures, how do we go about measuring the more important dimension of quality? Many experts argue that when quality is adequately taken into account, the productivity comparison among the United States, Japan, and Germany is even less favorable to the United States.

Productivity is a ratio; it is output divided by input. National productivity is important to each of us because it has a major impact on living standards. Material living standards can be measured in many ways, but perhaps the simplest and most valid is per capita gross domestic product (GDP), which is the gross domestic product of a country divided by its total population. This figure indicates the goods and services produced that would be available for consumption by every man, woman, and child if the goods and services were divided equally among them. A few years ago, the United States had the world's highest living standard by this index. At the present time, we rank no higher than eleventh—behind Switzerland, Finland, Sweden, Denmark, Norway, Japan, Germany, Luxembourg, Iceland, and Kuwait.

Why have we fallen so far behind? It is primarily because, for a number of years, our rate of productivity improvement has lagged behind that of other developed countries. In the long run there is no practical way that we can improve our standard of living relative to that of other countries except by improving productivity.

At the level of the individual enterprise, productivity is a basic competitive element. Obviously then, there are major advantages to improving productivity. At the national level, productivity improvement will enable us to increase our living standards in the United States; and at the level of the individual organization, it will enable the organization to be more competitive and thus provide greater rewards to its stakeholders (owners, executives, and production workers alike).

At the level of the individual enterprise, there are many ways to improve productivity, including increased investment in research and development, increased investment in plant and equipment, applications of new technology including robotics, and the many applications of computer technology to all kinds of work. But in the typical organization, the largest *unexplored* opportunity for improving productivity lies in the more effective utilization of people. Some companies that have concentrated attention on meeting the needs of employees as a major corporate strategy for improving productivity have found that they cannot merely achieve productivity improvements of 10 or 20 percent, but can, in fact, realize improvements of 200 percent or even higher.

One example of what can be done to improve the use of human resources can be seen in an experiment conducted at Kaiser Aluminum's plant in Ravenswood, West Virginia. Maintenance costs and tardiness fell when this company removed time clocks and permitted workers to supervise themselves and decide what machines to service and when. This program was implemented through the labor contract without resistance from the union concerned (the United Steelworkers of America). Kaiser Aluminum found that the maintenance function that was studied improved significantly in terms of quality, uptime, and costs (which went down 5.5 percent). Supervisory costs also decreased because a number of supervisory positions could be eliminated once the workers had more responsibility.

THE CHANGING WORKFORCE

The culture and social order of the United States have changed drastically since the early 1970s, and, not surprisingly, the new social values have been adopted by many in the workforce. More and more people are graduating from high school, going to college, and receiving advanced degrees. Although that is not the case at all levels of the workforce, the change is pronounced among managerial employees, engineers, and research and development employees, many of whom are now highly educated. What is equally important, many middle managers and first-level supervisors now have college degrees, and many blue-collar workers just joining the workforce now have high school diplomas (or even a few years of college).

Moreover, the workforce is becoming more knowledgeable and more sophisticated in general because of its exposure to the media. As society becomes better informed, however, it also becomes more critical, less willing to accept authority, and more cynical. This change in attitude, which is particularly prevalent among younger workers, is evident at all levels of the workforce—from executives and middle managers to blue-collar workers.

This increasing sophistication is both an advantage and a challenge to management. One of the challenges of the next twenty years will be to deal with a workforce that has a diverse, rather than a homogeneous, set of values. And, as already indicated, the challenge will come mainly from the younger workers.

As for changes in the values themselves, one of the most notable has been a general decline in the belief in the work ethic. There was a time when most people believed that work was inherently good. Few would deny that this belief has made our present affluence possible. That, however, was the ethic of a frontier society. Today we are witnessing the rise of a consumption ethic of an economically advanced society. Instead of emphasizing equality of opportunity and the value of hard work, we now appear to be demanding equality of results. Whether one approves of the emerging pattern or not, society rather than the individual is being asked to assume greater responsibility for providing both a minimum standard and a constantly increasing standard of living for all its members.

Another important change in the workforce that has a bearing on management strategy is the shifting balance between manual workers and knowledge workers. During the 1970s the U.S. economy passed a significant milestone when manual workers, who earn their living by job skill, became outnumbered for the first time in any society by knowledge workers, whose work depends on mental skills rather than physical skills and whose productivity is directly related to their formal education. Peter Drucker (1973, p. 241), for example, has pointed out that "This historic shift in the nature of work makes

Theory Y a necessity. The knowledge worker simply does not produce under *Theory X*. Knowledge has to be self-directed; the knowledge worker has to take responsibility."

Furthermore, the workers who are more highly trained appear to identify more strongly with their professional or occupational groups and thus are more loyal to the norms and values of those groups than to their employers. As a result, the workforce has become more mobile as the ties with a particular employer grow weaker.

There is also an intense desire for increased participation in decision making, increased control over job factors, and a greater voice in how the company is run. In turn, these changes, as noted earlier, are related to underlying social change. As such, they are part of a long-term trend that will persist well into the twenty-first century and thus must be kept in mind by those designing management systems.

Another fundamental trend today is the increasing frequency of midlife career changes. It is becoming common for individuals (both managers and blue-collar workers) to make dramatic shifts in their career patterns: executives enter the priesthood, engineers and scientists go into small businesses, and blue-collar workers leave their trades to go to college and enter new professional careers. These changes are now generally taken for granted by society.

Society's acceptance of midlife career changes, combined with the greater knowledge required in most occupations, has given rise to a new view of education as a lifetime pursuit. The rapid development of company-sponsored training and development programs, the increased attendance of both blue-collar and managerial workers in part-time college courses while employed, and the pursuit of MBA degrees in the evening by experienced executives all attest to this new trend, which will surely increase in intensity. In the twenty-first century, most members of the workforce will take for granted that they will go to school part time while they are working.

THE RESEARCH EVIDENCE: PEOPLE AND FINANCIAL PERFORMANCE

A considerable amount of empirical research indicates that several human resource management (HRM) practices help to increase worker productivity, performance, and job satisfaction. What the most effective of these practices seem to have in common is a concern for individual employee needs and goals. This was a main theme of the popular but controversial book *In Search of Excellence*. In their study of the management practices of the most successful companies in the United States (among them, Delta Air Lines, Johnson & Johnson, McDonald's, Texas Instruments), Peters and Waterman (1982) concluded that "attention to employees" is one of the main factors behind productivity. More recently, other researchers (notably, Kotter and Heskett, 1992; Pfeffer, 1994; Huselid, 1994) have documented similar findings.

The relationship among management practice, organization culture, and performance has been of considerable interest to researchers and to the business community for some time. Much of the early discussion, however, was based on conjecture and informal case studies. In the last few years, there has been a substantial increase in formal, empirical studies attempting to identify and describe the linkages among the concepts. Understanding the nature and direction of the relationships and how the underlying energies can be harnessed, focused, and controlled has important implications for productivity and business results.

An earlier study (Schuster, 1986) of the 1000 largest industrial and 300 largest nonindustrial firms in the United States found a significant relationship between employee-centered management practices and the financial performance of firms. Other studies (Blackburn and Rosen, 1993; Lawler, 1986, 1992) have strongly supported the role of employee involvement in achieving improved organizational performance. Mark Huselid (1994) has recently reported similar results.

Edward Lawler (1986, 1992), a particularly influential researcher in this field, concludes that the key to organizational effectiveness lies in completely changing the way organizations are managed. In order to be competitive, organizations will require highly skilled, knowledgeable workers and a relatively stable workforce. Traditional hierarchies must be transformed into organizations in which individuals know more, do more, and contribute more. This high-involvement or employee-centered management model is based on the belief that people can be trusted to make important decisions about the management of their work. This approach puts knowledge, power, rewards, and a communications network in place at every level in an organization. It encourages employees to care about the work they do, to know how to do it, and to do it as well as it can possibly be done. It is important to note, according to Lawler (1992), that the real basis for competitive advantage lies in the management systems that create and sustain this environment.

In a seminal study, John Kotter and James Heskett (1992) examined the relationship between organization culture and long-term economic performance across more than 200 organizations. In addition to being one of the largest and most rigorous research efforts to date on this subject, the study has made three important contributions. First, the relationship between culture and performance demonstrated in their studies is compelling. Second, the authors provide an important synthesis of theoretical viewpoints about the nature of culture. Third, they draw strong connections between management practices, culture, and performance. On the basis of their studies, Kotter and Heskett conclude:

1. Corporate culture can have a significant impact on a firm's long-term economic performance.
2. Corporate culture will probably be an even more important factor in determining the success or failure of firms in the next decade.
3. Corporate cultures that inhibit strong financial performance are not rare; they develop easily, even in firms that are full of reasonable and intelligent people.
4. Although tough to change, corporate cultures can be made more performance-enhancing.

Jeffrey Pfeffer, in a particularly important recent book (1994), has summarized very insightfully the current state of knowledge regarding the relationship of management practice, organization culture, and organization performance. Pfeffer identifies sixteen interrelated management practices that are shown by substantial research data to be significant determinants of superior financial performance in organizations:

- Employment security
- Selectivity in recruiting
- High wages
- Incentive pay
- Employee ownership
- Information sharing
- Participation and empowerment
- Teams and job redesign
- Training and skill development
- Cross-utilization and cross-training
- Symbolic egalitarianism
- Wage compression

- Promotion from within
- Long-term perspective
- Measurement of the practices
- Overarching philosophy

Pfeffer observes that, contrary to popular wisdom about fads in management, the basic ideas of how to manage people most effectively have remained remarkably stable over time. For example, the exceptional 80-year success story of Lincoln Electric Company and the more recent spectacular rise of Southwest Airlines can both be traced directly to the adoption of Douglas McGregor's Theory Y principles emphasizing confidence in the potential of individual employees to contribute to organization performance. While implementation details must be contingent on specific organization and industry conditions, the principles are fundamental and universal.

Pfeffer points out that, in the 20-year time period of 1972 to 1992, the five stocks that provided the greatest total return to stockholders were, in order, Plenum Publishing, Circuit City, Tyson Foods, Wal-Mart, and Southwest Airlines. These firms are all in industries characterized by massive competition that by conventional economic or strategic analysis would not be predicted to produce the most profitable results. The one thing these five firms have in common, however, is that for their sustained competitive advantage they rely on how they manage their workforce. For example, Southwest Airlines' competitive advantage comes primarily from its highly motivated and very productive workforce. Compared to other airlines, it has fewer employees per aircraft, flies more passengers per employee, and turns around 80 percent of its flights in 15 minutes or less instead of the industry average of 45 minutes. Southwest has also won the airlines' triple crown (best on-time performance, fewest bags lost, and fewest passenger complaints) far more times than any other airline.

As a result of this mounting research evidence and the positive experience of pathfinder firms, more and more companies in the United States are turning to employee-centered management—to enhance productivity and quality, and to gain the competitive advantage of a workforce fully committed to the organization's goals. Organizations are increasingly recognizing that efforts to improve productivity and quality must include attention to the human organization—its motivation, commitment, and morale. For example, a major component of the scoring system for the

Malcolm Baldrige Award involves accounting for the state of the human organization.

Increased attention is therefore being paid to developing tools for analysis and strategic management. These tools may be used for measuring the condition of the human organization, evaluating its performance, and initiating corrective action when needed to bring performance in line with organizational objectives. A number of leading firms including General Electric, Texas Instruments, and Motorola have pioneered the development of survey systems that facilitate such measurement.

Although numerous studies have consistently shown a significant relationship between employee-centered management practices and excellent organizational performance, executives rightly conclude that proving the effectiveness of a practice in one particular setting does not mean it will be equally effective in a variety of settings. What is needed is supplementary evidence based on experience in a cross-section of diverse organizations to determine if the use of employee-centered management practices leads to superior financial performance.

The author has conducted a large-scale validation study of the relationship between the use of employee-centered management practices and an authoritative criterion of organizational effectiveness (that is, *Fortune* magazine's annual figures on financial performance). Six practices were the focus of the research: the assessment-center approach to personnel selection; flexible reward systems; productivity bonus plans; goal-oriented performance appraisal; alternative work schedules; and organizational development. Although other practices could have been included, these were selected because they were thought to be closest to the primary concern of the study, which was a general management philosophy, and could therefore serve as an operational definition of the philosophy (that is, the greater the number of such practices being used, the more "people-oriented" the corporate management's philosophy). Forty-six percent of the 1,000 largest industrial and 300 largest nonindustrial companies in the United States participated in the research.

The total number of the six practices utilized was correlated with a composite criterion of return on equity and change in return on equity. The study showed conclusively that *a statistically significant relationship exists between the use of the employee-centered management practices and superior financial performance.* Further, when the firms using the practices were compared with those not using them, the average return on equity of the firms using one or more of the six innovative practices was 11 percent higher than the return of those firms not using any of the practices. When the correlation shown here is viewed alongside the numerous experimental and case studies presented earlier, the evidence for the effectiveness of employee-centered management is quite substantial.

The most plausible explanation for these findings is that a greater number of employee-centered management practices in place reflects an underlying strong interest in the human resources of the organization and in the motivation and optimum utilization of those resources. In other words, the use of many employee-centered practices reflects a *qualitative* difference in the attitude of the organization toward its employees. This difference in attitude and emphasis, rather than the number of practices utilized, is almost certainly the significant factor. These findings should draw management's attention to the value of employee-centered management in corporate strategy.

WHAT EMPLOYEES SAY ABOUT MANAGEMENT PRACTICES

Previous research (Schuster, 1986) using an employee survey instrument called the *Human Resources Index (HRI)* provides insight into the views of employees concerning various management practices. When questioned about 15 factors in their work situation, several thousand employees in a cross section of more than 40 diverse organizations stated that they were least satisfied with the opportunity they had to participate in the decision making of the organization. The complaint most often voiced was that they did not get enough information about the business objectives, goals, and plans of the organization. Employees were also relatively dissatisfied with their reward systems (perhaps this matches the preconception of many executives). However, it was *not* the absolute level of rewards offered that bothered them, but the relative *distribution* of rewards within their organizations. Although many of the organizations concerned professed to have "merit" pay plans, most of their employees believed that pay was not closely related to individual performance and contribution.

Perhaps the most important conclusion that can be drawn from the *HRI* research is that such a survey can be used to evaluate how effectively an organization is managing its people. Moreover, the survey data have proved helpful in diagnosing specific problems and in initiating organization development by opening up two-way communication about matters of practical significance to the organization.

ATTENTION TO EMPLOYEES AND PERFORMANCE

Numerous individual firms have demonstrated that the use of "attention to employees" as a major corporate strategy leads to superior financial performance. The *Wall Street Journal* has reported that the miners at the Southern Utah Fuel Company (SUFCO), a small coal mining company located in Convulsion Canyon, Utah, "dig an astounding 2½ times more coal per man per day than is dug in the average underground coal mine in the U.S." Needless to say, the company is highly profitable even though *starting* pay for miners, including incentive bonuses, comes to more than $30,000 a year. Furthermore, absenteeism and turnover are reported to be practically nonexistent and the mine is said to be union-proof. The company's emphasis on "attention to employees" and the lack of any barriers between management and the workers appear to be the main reasons for this organization's highly effective performance. Hewlett-Packard, Motorola, Donnelly Mirrors (Donnelly Corporation), and Delta Air Lines also experience very low rates of absenteeism and turnover and high levels of performance as a result of employee-centered management.

The success demonstrated by these companies has been matched and even surpassed by that of Japanese firms such as Honda, Sony, and YKK Zipper in their U.S. plants. In these plants, Japanese executives are using essentially Japanese management practices with American workers. Although the Japanese are technically skilled in many areas of management, their greatest competitive advantage, they believe, is the closeness and cooperation between executives and employees achieved through the de-emphasis of status differences (such as executive dinning rooms, private offices, or reserved parking), emphasis on communication, and attention to employee needs.

WHAT JAPAN HAS LEARNED ABOUT MANAGEMENT FROM THE UNITED STATES

There is a common misconception in America that the theories behind participative management and other styles of management that emphasize meeting the needs of employees have been imported from Japan. This myth has been furthered by a number of books that have applauded the success (quite appropriately) of the Japanese in implementing these management styles and using them effectively in order to achieve high productivity. But it is incorrect to infer that the Japanese developed these approaches to management or were responsible for their theoretical underpinnings. In fact, nothing could be further from the truth. American behavioral researchers and industrial psychologists led the way in this development, beginning with the Hawthorne Studies at the Western Electric Company in the late 1920s. The real giants in this field have all been Americans: Elton Mayo and Fritz Roethlisberger, who conducted the Hawthorne Studies; Douglas McGregor, who taught at MIT and wrote the classic book *The Human Side of Enterprise*; Rensis Likert of the University of Michigan, who pioneered in the use of attitude measurement as a strategic tool; and Chris Argyris of Yale and Harvard, who pointed out the shortcomings of traditional approaches to managing people. Although all of these pioneers and giants are Americans, the tragedy is that until very recently they have been largely ignored in America, whereas their works have been studied and memorized by the Japanese and form the theoretical basis for what we now think as of the "Japanese management style."

The fact is that the typical Japanese executive is a much more avid reader of American management literature, including both major management books and the better management periodicals, than his or her American counterpart. Practically every American management book of any consequence is quickly translated into Japanese and is avidly read in Japan, and the typical Japanese executive regularly reads several American management periodicals. And so when we read of innovative Japanese management practices such as quality circles, decision making by consensus, removal of such barriers to communication as isolated offices and executive dining rooms, and emphasis on personal contact through management-by-walking-around, we should always keep in mind that these concepts have their origin in American management thought. What the Japanese should be admired for, however, is their willingness to study and to learn these approaches, their daring in actually putting them into practice in order to test them out, and their perseverance in making them work. In many ways the Japanese have done us a great service by taking the risk to demonstrate that these practices do work, and that they can pay off handsomely in impressive productivity.

The degree to which the Japanese are avid students of American management theory was dramatically brought home to me by a personal experience early in my career. In the late 1960s, fresh out of a graduate degree program at the Harvard Business School, I found myself in a junior staff position with a major New York management consulting firm. One day, fairly early in my tenure with this firm, I was asked to coordinate and host the visit of a delegation of high-level Japanese executives who were touring the United States and spending time visiting their counterparts in major American corporations and a small number of consulting firms. Probably because I was so recently out of an academic program, I was asked by the partners in my firm to meet with the group of Japanese executives during their one-day visit and to discuss with them the work of major management theorists such as McGregor, Likert, and Argyris. The Japanese had actually prepared a list of American management theorists that they wanted to discuss, and in retrospect this probably should have alerted me to check more carefully into their level of knowledge. But at the time I knew nothing about Japanese management practices or Japanese management education. I puzzled for several days over how to present in a short period of time to a group of executives from a completely different culture the essence of the research and managerial thought that, after all, had taken approximately 40 years to develop in America. As events were to prove, I was worrying about the wrong things.

As I began my presentation I described the famous Hawthorne Studies done at Western Electric's plant in the 1920s and 1930s, and outlined the revolutionary notion coming from these studies that the culture created within a work group can massively impact the output of the group, and that culture in fact can be far more important than either technology or physical working conditions. I then went on to describe some of the basic elements of Douglas McGregor's Theory Y, and Rensis Likert's Systems I, II, III, and IV. The Japanese listened very quietly and very patiently. They seemed interested, even fascinated, and nobody interrupted. Instead, they all listened politely as I concluded my rather elementary presentation. When I did finally pause and ask if there were questions, there was a polite silence for a few moments and then one executive said (through a translator), "Well actually we have prepared a number of questions that we would like to discuss with you. For example, we have all noted what Douglas McGregor says on page 'a' (about halfway down the page) . . . ; but we are puzzled by this because it seems to contradict what he says on page 'b' (the third line from the bottom)." They then proceeded with a list of similar questions that would have embarrassed any panel of American doctoral students or scholars, let alone practicing managers. Some of these executives could literally quote whole pages from memory and obviously not only had digested the nuances of the theories but had done a great deal of critical analysis.

I clearly recall the impression at the time that if these executives were typical, the Japanese were probably about to overtake us by using our own management theory against us. I must admit, however, that it was only a fleeting thought to which I paid little attention; I certainly could never have imagined where the careful application of American management theory would lead the Japanese by the 1990s: literally to conquering America's leadership industries—automobiles, consumer electronics, and steel. Who would have imagined 25 years ago that the Japanese could seriously challenge the American automobile industry, which had dominated the world since the invention of the automobile?

U.S. FIRMS HAVE BEEN SLOW TO ADOPT PROGRESSIVE MANAGEMENT PRACTICES

Despite the clearly superior financial performance of firms utilizing innovative HRM practices, HRM technology still has not been widely applied in the United States. It seems reasonable to ask, "Why has American business and industry been so reluctant, at least so slow, to adopt progressive HRM practices when improved performance is so obviously needed?" The reasons are complex:

1. Complacency and inertia. *Until recently* many executives never questioned or considered changing the status quo, which they found to be fairly comfortable.
2. Lack of hard data indicating which practices are effective and under what conditions (that is, the contingent considerations).
3. Short time-span focus of management systems in general, and reward systems in particular. Performance bonuses, promotion, and contributions to retirement plans are often tied to performance in one year, rather than to building a committed workforce (which is a long-term task).
4. Lack of *measurement* of HRM practices. Until recently, little attention has been paid to executive performance regarding

effective utilization of human resources, in part because accurate measurement was not possible and standards for comparison did not exist. What is indeed remarkable is our lack of *control* over the efficient utilization of the most expensive single cost of operation in many organizations.

5. Management's reluctance to give up special status, privileges, and perquisites. Executive dining rooms, private offices, better furniture, executive washrooms, country club memberships, reserved parking spaces, differences in dress, being called "Mr." instead of "Joe"—all are treasured status symbols to executives. They have a significant psychological reward value. By *definition*, these things also *separate* people—make others in the organization feel less important, less needed, less influential. They block communication, inhibit participation, restrict motivation and contribution. Is this becoming too high a price for the organization to pay?

The fact is that innovation in management has not kept pace with changes in technology or products. Managements that take pride in being at the leading edge in developing new products or in introducing new manufacturing technology are hopelessly mired in management practices that have changed little since the 1930s—and they are *extremely reluctant to experiment*. What they need to do is commit themselves to a concrete strategy for improving productivity through employee-centered management. I am going to suggest such a strategy which, with appropriate adaptation, will fit the needs of a great many organizations. Because this strategy is based on the experience and practice of some of the most effective and financially successful firms in America, it is referred to here as *Strategy A*.

Strategy A is a structured process to change the culture of an organization from one of management by direction and control (Theory X) to one of management by commitment and self-control (Theory Y).

STRATEGY A: SEVEN STEPS TO IMPROVED PRODUCTIVITY AND PERFORMANCE

1. *Determine the baseline condition of the human organization using a validated and standardized survey instrument.* Many executives believe that they can sense whether the morale of the

organization is high or low, but this is seldom the case. In a recent study of a large bank, for example, the CEO was elated to discover that the teller group had a much higher level of morale and commitment to the organization than he had believed. On the other hand, he was appalled to discover that the top officers were among the most dissatisfied.

2. *Use the survey data to identify and act on key opportunities for improvement—that is, identify cost-effective "winners" worthy of special attention because of a high payout/investment ratio.* Some likely candidates that will surface in many organizations are:

   a. Improve communication, especially where organization goals and objectives are concerned. Commenting on Motorola's Participative Management Program, an executive in that company recently said, "Our people expect to live in a rational world. That means if management plans and decisions are seen as rational and reasonable, people can and will work more effectively. Employees are more effective when they are aware of their company's goals and performance."

   b. Increase participation of rank-and-file employees in important management decisions. At Harman International, production workers participate in planning bids for new contracts. As a result, they have found that the ability to make really tight bids, and then stay under budgeted costs, gives them an important competitive edge. At Donnelly Mirrors (Donnelly Corporation), work teams determine their own pay. The results of this process are posted and are subject to challenge by other teams. General Electric has reported on a new grievance review process in a *nonunion* facility in which the controlling majority of the grievance panel (with authority to bind the company) is made up of rank-and-file production employees. These management practices may alarm some executives, but the point is, *they work.*

   c. Rationalize the *distribution* of rewards by linking pay and other rewards directly to performance. Kopelman et al. (1983, p. 79) have reported that at a large financial institution "Those branches with a strong tie between performance and rewards achieved significantly higher levels of performance than did those branches with a weak tie between performance and rewards." Numerous studies have illustrated that pay is by far the most powerful incentive to improve work performance.

d. Implement a flexible compensation program that allows each employee to choose compensation and fringe benefits on the basis of personal preferences and obligations. This approach ensures full motivational value for every dollar spent on compensation and benefits. Commenting on American Can Company's pioneering cafeteria plan, Sal Giudice (personal communication) says:

> From the perspective of more than five years of experience, it's clear to us at American Can that flexible benefits *are* successful, but not the final answer. We now see flexible benefits as only the first step in the evolution of a completely flexible compensation program which will permit employees to trade off between benefits and pay. This program eventually will include other areas, such as hours worked, career options, and ultimately, every aspect of the employee work environment. A comprehensive survey showed that American Can's Flexible Benefits Program is extremely popular among our employees—89 percent like being able to select new benefits each year. Perhaps most significant, flexible benefits permit a company to respond to unique needs of employees in a *cost effective* fashion.

e. Consider adopting a productivity bonus plan that allows employees to share tangibly and directly in the improved financial results from *their* successful efforts to increase productivity. The principle here is quite simple. If you want people to increase productivity, pay them for it. Lincoln Electric Company has for years had an exceptionally successful program for linking compensation directly to improved organizational performance. As a part of the Federal government's effort to stimulate improved productivity, the U.S. General Accounting Office (GAO) conducted a comprehensive study of all firms identified as having installed productivity gains-sharing programs. The GAO research concluded that:

> The performance of the productivity sharing plans studied suggests that these plans offer a viable method of enhancing productivity. While productivity sharing plans are not a panacea for every firm or the solution to the Nation's economic problems, they warrant serious consideration by firms as a means of stimulating productivity performance, enhancing their employees, and reducing inflationary pressures. Many of the firms included in our study achieved significant savings from their productivity sharing plans and also enjoyed many nonmonetary benefits. Firms that provided financial information on the results of their plans *averaged* savings of almost

17 percent in work force cost. Other benefits attributed to the plan included improved labor-management relations, reduced absenteeism and turnover, and fewer grievances.

3. *Change executive evaluation and reward practices to measure and pay for effective management of people as well as the traditional measures of profit, productivity, cost, and so on.* If executives are to build the human organization over the long term, we have to measure this performance and include it in pay determination. We have to learn to invest for the long term in people as well as equipment. We must move toward measuring performance by long-term results instead of year to year and we need to commit our organizations to sacrifice short-term profits for long-term control of markets.

4. *Remove artificial barriers to participation, communication, and contribution.* Such barriers include separate dining rooms, reserved parking spaces, elaborate office space and furnishings that exceed actual work requirements, and other unnecessary status symbols. Careful evaluation of these practices may indicate that they are anachronisms, appropriate perhaps to another era, but that have now outlived their usefulness. As Bill Machaver (personal communication) of Sun Chemical puts it,

Employees today have a different background and mentality; they are truly a new breed; they don't think the manager is automatically the enemy. They are interested in job security, better quality of life and better family life. And most importantly, they are ready and willing to work with management to achieve these goals by cooperation rather than confrontation.

5. *Report to employees what has been done to change management assumptions and practices, and solicit their participation in planning further change.* This is one way of directly implementing participative management. Consider, for example, the response when one company's CEO announced, "In last year's employee survey over 70 percent of you asked for more information on company goals and objectives, so we are starting to distribute a monthly status report on corporate objectives and new business plans. Moreover, we are actively seeking the ideas of everyone in the organization for product improvements and new product applications." The excitement that ensued was both immediate and obvious.

6. *Measure again the condition of the human organization using the same standardized survey instrument to determine changes.* Repeat this standardized measurement of human resources annually.
   a. Use this measure as an evaluation tool for managers.
   b. Feed data back to employees at all levels of the organization. Involve elected teams of employees representing all functional areas in analyzing and interpreting the data to generate recommendations for further improvement. Although review teams may be advisory only, top management should agree to give their views a great deal of weight.
7. *Measure the correlation between the survey data and hard criteria of organizational performance—productivity, profitability, growth, costs, and so on.* Use this information to reinforce the productivity improvement strategy and to modify it if necessary.

Growing evidence indicates that employee-centered management will have a great impact on organizations during the next two decades. Companies that begin to manage their human organization effectively will forge ahead, whereas those that do not will be unable to remain competitive. If this seems an overly harsh prediction, consider the fate of the troubled airline in Chapter 1. In the future, organizational success will increasingly depend on harnessing untapped potential in the workforce for commitment to the goals of the organization.

These changes will require a contingency approach to managing human resources that departs from the assumption that all people have the same needs and expectations and can, therefore, be managed in the same way, through the same policies. Rather, the contingency approach assumes the opposite. It assumes that people differ in terms of the needs that motivate them, in terms of the managerial styles and policies to which they will respond, and in terms of the kind of organizational environment in which they can be most effective.

Although the central task for American business—increasing productivity—will require effort on many fronts, including breakthroughs in manufacturing technology, robotics, and use of microcomputers, for the majority of companies the best opportunity for improving productivity—one currently untapped—lies in the more effective use of people.

Fortunately, the technology for effective management of the human organization is already at hand; the problem is to implement what we already know. Although the Japanese have been credited with inventing employee-centered management, it was really "made in America." As Kyosuke Mori of Mitsubishi International says, "I don't think there is anything we know that the Americans don't know. If we are doing something right in managing our business, we have learned it from the Americans. It is ironical that the Americans are now talking about our management technique as though it is some kind of secret weapon that we are using against them. The underlying principles and philosophies are American." Furthermore, employee-centered management has been applied in America with spectacular and carefully documented success by such organizations as Motorola, Hewlett-Packard, Walt Disney, Donnelly Mirrors (Donnelly Corporation), and many others.

Does this mean that attention to employees is by itself a panacea for achieving excellent organizational performance? Of course not; it can serve only as an enhancer of other managerial strategies. But the overwhelming evidence from studies in individual firms is that effective management of people can work as a powerful amplifier of the benefits from other efforts to improve productivity, such as better quality control, increased investment in research and development, and technological innovation.

On the basis of the accumulating evidence, it appears that employee-centered management is going to have a major impact on organizations during the next two decades. Companies that begin to manage their human resources effectively will forge ahead because they will be harnessing the untapped potential for commitment to the goals of the organization. Other companies will find they are unable to remain competitive.

The technology of Strategy A consists of creating those conditions within the organization that make it possible for individuals to contribute 100 percent (or nearly so) of their potential value to the organization rather than 50 percent, or 40 percent, or even less.

Strategy A may be viewed by some as "idealistic," but it is as realistic as dollars and cents can be. Because the American economic system places a premium on performance and "whatever works," Strategy A's wide-scale adoption is inevitable, as was the adoption of automation and information technology.

Although this book emphasizes a contingency approach, fitting specific management systems to the particular circumstances and needs of each individual organization, it also proposes a prescriptive model for a systematic motivation-oriented approach to managing for high productivity. This prescriptive model (Strategy A) is research-based, synthesizing those innovative practices that are working effectively for a high percentage of the *Fortune* 1300 firms using them.

The objectives of Strategy A can be summed up best in these words of Peter Drucker: "In the better use of human resources lies the major opportunity for increasing productivity. . . . Management of people should be the first and foremost concern of operating management, rather than the management of things."

3 THE THEORY BEHIND STRATEGY A

There is a chain of American research and theory that provides the theoretical underpinnings for Strategy A, and that the Japanese have adapted so effectively to forge their economic miracle. Excerpts from the original writing of Homans, McGregor, and Likert will demonstrate that the successful management practices of Hewlett-Packard, Motorola, Donnelly Mirrors (Donnelly Corporation), and other companies, as well as the prescriptions of Strategy A, are based directly on the work of these theorists.

THE HAWTHORNE STUDIES AND THE BIRTH OF A NEW IDEA

The Hawthorne Studies were a series of research studies carried out during the decade from the mid-1920s to the mid-1930s at the Hawthorne (Chicago) works of the Western Electric Company. Among the researchers who participated in the conduct of the research and the interpretation of the data were Elton Mayo, Fritz J. Roethlisberger, T.N. Whitehead, W.J. Dickson, and George C. Homans.

These studies stretched over a number of years and consisted of many separate experiments. They started out as rather straightforward industrial engineering research to determine optimum lighting for an assembly operation and optimum rest pauses for the assemblers. Such research had been performed before, and the

Hawthorne Studies were initially viewed as only a new attempt to determine the optimum physical conditions for high productivity. In one phase of the studies the illumination of the workplace was varied experimentally, and the productivity that resulted under various conditions of illumination was measured. First, the illumination would be raised from the beginning point and productivity would be measured, then illumination would be lowered and productivity measured; the productivity measures were collected over a period of time. The original assumption of the studies was that eventually a pattern would emerge that would show the optimum level of illumination.

Similarly, another series of studies examined the effect of rest pauses on productivity. As changes were made in the schedule of rest pauses, productivity was measured. At some points there were two pauses of short duration in the morning and two of short duration in the afternoon; at other times there was one longer pause in the morning and a longer pause in the afternoon; and so on. Under some experimental conditions, the workday was lengthened or shortened. Again, it was assumed that, over a period of time, a pattern of correlation would emerge so that it would be possible to determine the optimum schedule of rest pauses in order to maximize productivity.

To the astonishment of the experimenters, in none of the research did the expected pattern emerge. In fact, at first there appeared to be no pattern to the result. Incredibly, it appeared that no matter what change was made, productivity went up. If the light was increased, productivity went up; but when the light was decreased, it went up again. When rest pauses were increased, productivity went up; but when they were taken away, productivity, instead of going down as the researchers expected, went up again. In fact, the only pattern that the researchers could observe was that at each experimental stage the productivity was higher than at the previous one.

The researchers recognized that something much more powerful than physical conditions was intervening in the experiment and confounding the results, but it took many years of analysis to realize what had actually been happening. Eventually it was concluded that a set of conditions had been created that had completely revolutionized the relationship of the employees to each other and to the organization. The experimental conditions, which isolated the workers and gave them great freedom to interact with each other, had caused them to form a social group.

Because of the total work situation and the positive relationship with the superintendent of the Hawthorne works, the employees developed among themselves the norm of a high level of productivity. They wanted the experiment to succeed and thus they decided that, no matter what conditions were changed, they would aim to work more productively. Even when they complained of such physical difficulties as mugginess or heat, these conditions were not apparently affecting their output. Of course, if the lights had been turned out entirely, or if the heat had become so intense that heat prostration had resulted, productivity would have been negatively affected. But within the limits in which these conditions were varied in the experimental situation, the physical conditions such as light, heat, rest pauses, and so forth appeared to have no effect on the rate of output.

On the other hand, the social development of the work group, its development over time of positive norms aligned with organizational objectives, and the development of a positive relationship with the company executive in charge of the experimental group appeared to bear a very direct relationship to the level of output.

The conclusions from the Hawthorne Studies are perhaps best described by George C. Homans:[1]

The question remains: with what facts, if any, can the changes in the output rate of the operators in the test room be correlated? Here the statement of the [operators] themselves are of first importance. Each knew that she was producing more in the test room than she ever had in the regular department, and each said that the increase had come about without any conscious effort on her part. It seemed easier to produce at the faster rate in the test room than at the slower rate in the regular department. When questioned further, each [operator] stated her reasons in slightly different words, but there was uniformity in the answers in two respects. First, the [operators] liked to work in the test room; "it was fun." Secondly, the new supervisory control made it possible for them to work freely without anxiety.

For instance, there was the matter of conversation. In the regular department, conversation was in principle not allowed. In practice it was tolerated if it was carried on in a low tone and did not interfere with work. In the test room an effort was made in the beginning to discourage conversation, though it was soon abandoned. The observer in charge of the experiment was afraid of losing the cooperation of the [operators] if he insisted too strongly on this point. Talk became common and was often loud and general. Indeed the conversation of the operators came to occupy an important place in the log. T.N. Whitehead has pointed out that the [operators] in the test room were far more thoroughly supervised than they ever had been in the regular department. They were watched by an observer of their own, an interested management, and outside experts. The point is that the character and purpose of the supervision were different and were felt to be so. The operators knew that they were taking part in what was considered an important and interesting experiment. They knew that their work was expected to produce results—they were not sure what results—which would lead to the improvement of the working conditions of their fellow employees. They knew that the eyes of the company were upon them.

Whitehead has further pointed out that, although the experimental changes might turn out to have no physical significance, their social significance was always favorable. They showed that the management of the company was still interested, that the [operators] were still part of a valuable piece of research. In the regular department they, like the other employees, were in the position of responding to changes the source and purpose of which were beyond their knowledge. In the test room they had frequent interviews with the superintendent, a high officer of the company. The reasons for the contemplated experimental changes were explained to them. Their views were consulted and in some instances they were allowed to veto what had been proposed. Professor Mayo has argued that it is idle to speak of an experimental period like Period XII as being in any sense what it purported to be—a return of the original conditions of work.

In the meantime, the entire industrial situation of the [operators] had been reconstructed. Before long they had committed themselves to a continuous increase in production. . . . In brief, the increase in the output rate in the Relay Assembly Test Room could not be related to any changes in the physical conditions of work, whether experimentally induced or not. It could, however, be related to what can only be spoken of as the development of an organized social group in a peculiar and effective relation with its supervisors.

Many of these conclusions were not worked out in detail until long after the investigators at Hawthorne had lost interest in the Relay Assembly Test Room, but the general meaning of the experiment was clear at least as early as Period XII. A continuous increase in productivity had taken place irrespective of changing physical conditions of work. In the words of a company report made in January, 1931, on all the research which had been done up to that date:

Upon analysis, only one thing seemed to show a continuous relationship with this improved output. This was the mental attitude of the operators. From their conversations with each other and their comments to the test observers, it was not only clear that their attitudes were improving but it was evident that this area of employee reactions and feeling was a fruitful field for industrial research.

The Hawthorne Studies thus gave birth to a new idea, the notion that the culture of a work group—in particular its norms or standards with regard to productivity and its attitude toward the organizational hierarchy—can profoundly affect the productivity of the group, with an impact probably much greater than that of technology, working conditions, or other such "external" variables.

DOUGLAS McGREGOR, THE PHILOSOPHER, AND THE VALUES OF STRATEGY A

Douglas McGregor, who is famous for his Theory X and Theory Y concepts of human nature, was among the first to suggest practical applications of the new findings about organizational culture that emerged from the Hawthorne Studies. McGregor claimed that old-line Theory X managers who believed that people inherently dislike work and must be coerced to do it are not as effective as Theory Y managers who believe that people are self-motivated, want to work, and can be encouraged best through trust and cooperation. Like Elton Mayo and George Homans, McGregor stressed the importance of cohesive working groups led by psychologically sophisticated managers who were able to create working conditions under which the emergent work norms of the group would be harmonious with the goals of the enterprise.

McGregor refers to Theory X as "the traditional view of management by direction and control," and he describes Theory X as follows:[2]

Behind every managerial decision or action are assumptions about human nature and human behavior. A few of these are remarkably pervasive. They are implicit in most of the literature of organization and in much current managerial policy and practice:

1. *The average human being has an inherent dislike of work and will avoid it if he can.* This assumption has deep roots. The punishment of Adam and Eve for eating the fruit of the Tree of Knowledge was to be banished from Eden into a world where they had to work for a living. The stress that management places on productivity, on the concept of "a fair day's work," on the evils of featherbedding and restriction of output, on rewards for performance—while it has a logic in terms of the objectives of enterprise—reflects an underlying belief that management must counteract an inherent human tendency to avoid work. The evidence for the correctness of the assumption would seem to most managers to be incontrovertible.

2. *Because of this human characteristic of dislike of work, most people must be coerced, controlled, directed, threatened with punishment to get them to put forth adequate effort toward the achievement of organizational*

objectives. The dislike of work is so strong that even the promise of rewards is not generally enough to overcome it. People will accept the rewards and demand continually higher ones, but these alone will not produce the necessary effort. Only the threat of punishment will do the trick.

3. *The average human being prefers to be directed, wishes to avoid responsibility, has relatively little ambition, wants security above all.* This assumption of the "mediocrity of the masses" is rarely expressed so bluntly. In fact, a good deal of lip service is given to the ideal of the worth of the average human being. Our political and social values demand such public expressions. Nevertheless, a great many managers will give private support to this assumption, and it is easy to see it reflected in policy and practice.

I have suggested elsewhere the name Theory X for this set of assumptions. . . . Theory X is not a straw man for purposes of demolition, but is in fact a theory which materially influences managerial strategy in a wide sector of American industry today. Moreover, the principles of organization which comprise the bulk of the literature of management *could only have been derived from assumptions such as those of Theory X.* Other beliefs about human nature would have led inevitably to quite different organizational principles.

Theory X provides an explanation of some human behavior in industry. These assumptions would not have persisted if there were not a considerable body of evidence to support them. Nevertheless, there are many readily observable phenomena in industry and elsewhere which are not consistent with this view of human nature.

The growth of knowledge in the social sciences during the past quarter century has made it possible to reformulate some assumptions about human nature and human behavior in the organizational setting which resolve certain of the inconsistencies inherent in Theory X. While this reformulation is, of course, tentative, it provides an improved basis for prediction and control of human behavior in industry. . . .

The philosophy of management by direction and control—*regardless of whether it is hard or soft*—is inadequate to motivate because the human needs on which this approach relies are relatively unimportant motivators of behavior in our society today. Direction and control are of limited value in motivating people whose important needs are social and egoistic.

People, deprived of opportunities to satisfy at work the needs which are now important to them, behave exactly as we might predict—with indolence, passivity, unwillingness to accept responsibility, resistance to change, willingness to follow the demagogue, unreasonable demands for economic benefits. It would seem that we may be caught in a web of our own weaving.

Theory X explains the *consequences* of a particular managerial strategy; it neither explains nor describes human nature although it purports to.

Because its assumptions are so unnecessarily limiting, it prevents our seeing the possibilities inherent in other managerial strategies. What sometimes appear to be new strategies—decentralization, management by objectives, consultative supervision, "democratic" leadership—are usually but old wine in new bottles because the procedures developed to implement them are derived from the same inadequate assumptions about human nature. Management is constantly becoming disillusioned with widely touted and expertly merchandised "new approaches" to the human side of enterprise. The real difficulty is that these new approaches are no more than different tactics—programs, procedures, gadgets—within an unchanged strategy based on Theory X.

Theory Y

Theory Y, which McGregor refers to as management by integration of individual and organizational goals, is described by McGregor as follows:[3]

There have been few dramatic breakthroughs in social science theory like those which have occurred in the physical sciences during the past half century. Nevertheless, the accumulation of knowledge about human behavior in many specialized fields has made possible the formulation of a number of generalizations which provide a modest beginning for new theory with respect to the management of human resources. Some of these generalizations, which will hereafter be referred to as Theory Y, are as follows:

1. *The expenditure of physical and mental effort in work is as natural as play or rest.* The average human being does not inherently dislike work. Depending on controllable conditions, work may be a source of satisfaction (and will be voluntarily performed) or a source of punishment (and will be avoided if possible).
2. *External control and the threat of punishment are not the only means for bringing about effort toward organizational objectives. Man will exercise self-direction and self-control in the service of objectives to which he is committed.*
3. *Commitment to objectives is a function of the rewards associated with their achievement.* The most significant of such rewards, the satisfaction of ego and self-actualization needs, can be direct products of effort directed toward organizational objectives.
4. *The average human being learns, under proper conditions, not only to accept but to seek responsibility.* Avoidance of responsibility, lack of ambition, and emphasis on security are generally consequences of experience, not inherent human characteristics.

5. *The capacity to exercise a relatively high degree of imagination, ingenuity, and creativity in the solution of organizational problems is widely, not narrowly, distributed in the population.*
6. *Under the conditions of modern industrial life, the intellectual potentialities of the average human being are only partially utilized.*

These assumptions involve sharply different implications for managerial strategy than do those of Theory X. They are dynamic rather than static: They indicate the possibility of human growth and development; they stress the necessity for selective adaptation rather than for a single absolute form of control. They are not framed in terms of the least common denominator of the factory hand, but in terms of a resource which has substantial potentialities.

Above all, *the assumptions of Theory Y point up the fact that the limits on human collaboration in the organizational setting are not limits of human nature but of management's ingenuity in discovering how to realize the potential represented by its human resources.* Theory X offers management an easy rationalization for ineffective organizational performance: It is due to the nature of the human resources with which we must work. Theory Y, on the other hand, places the problems squarely in the lap of management. If employees are lazy, indifferent, unwilling to take responsibility, intransigent, uncreative, uncooperative, Theory Y implies that the causes lie in management's methods of organization and control.

The Principle of Integration

The central principle of organization which derives from Theory X is that of direction and control through the exercise of authority—what has been called "the scalar principle." The central principle which derives from Theory Y is that of integration: the creation of conditions such that the members of the organization can achieve their own goals best by directing their efforts towards the success of the enterprise. These two principles have profoundly different implications with respect to the task of managing human resources, but the scalar principle is so firmly built into managerial attitudes that the implications of the principle of integration are not easy to perceive.

Someone once said that fish discover water last. The "psychological environment" of industrial management—like water for fish—is so much a part of organizational life that we are unaware of it. Certain characteristics of our society, and of organizational life within it, are so completely established, so pervasive, that we cannot conceive of their being otherwise. As a result, a great many policies and practices and decisions and relationships could only be—it seems—what they are.

Among these pervasive characteristics of organizational life in the United States today is a managerial attitude (stemming from Theory X) toward membership in the organization. It is assumed almost without question that organizational requirements take precedence over the needs of individual members. Basically, the employment agreement is that in return for the rewards which are offered, the individual will accept external direction and control. The very idea of integration and self-control is foreign to our way of thinking about the employment relationship.

The concept of integration and self-control carries the implication that the organization will be more effective in achieving its economic objectives if adjustments are made, in significant ways, to the needs and goals of its members:

> A district manager in a large, geographically decentralized company is notified that he is being promoted to a policy level position at headquarters. It is a big promotion with a large salary increase. His role in the organization will be a much more powerful one, and he will be associated with the major executives of the firm.
>
> The headquarters group who selected him for this position have carefully considered a number of possible candidates. This man stands out among them in a way which makes him the natural choice. His performance qualifies him not only for this opening but for an even higher position. There is genuine satisfaction that such an outstanding candidate is available.
>
> The man is appalled. He doesn't want the job. His goal, as he expresses it, is to be the "best damned district manager in the company." He enjoys his direct associations with operating people in the field and he doesn't want a policy level job. He and his wife enjoy the kind of life they have created in a small city, and they dislike actively both the living conditions and the social obligations of the headquarters city. He expresses his feelings as strongly as he can, but his objections are brushed aside. The organization's needs are such that his refusal to accept the promotion would be unthinkable. His superiors say to themselves that of course when he has settled into the new job, he will recognize that it was the right thing. And so he makes the move.
>
> Two years later he is in an even higher position in the company's headquarters organization, and there is talk that he will probably be the executive vice-president before long. Privately he expresses considerable unhappiness and dissatisfaction. He (and his wife) would "give anything" to be back in the situation he left two years ago.

Within the context of the pervasive assumptions of Theory X, promotions and transfers in large numbers are made by unilateral decision. The requirements of the organization are given priority automatically and almost without question. If the individual's personal goals are considered at all, it is assumed that the rewards of salary and position will satisfy him.

Should an individual actually refuse such a move without a compelling reason, such as health or a severe family crisis, he would be considered to have jeopardized his future because of his "selfish" attitude. It is rare indeed for a management to give the individual the opportunity to be a genuine and active partner in such a decision, even though it may affect his most important personal goals.

Yet the implications following from Theory Y are that the organization is likely to suffer if it ignores these personal needs and goals. In making unilateral decisions with respect to promotion, management is failing to utilize its human resources in the most effective way.

The principle of integration demands that both the organization's and the individual's needs be recognized. Of course, when there is a sincere joint effort to find it, an integrative solution which meets the needs of the individual *and* the organization is a frequent outcome. But not always — and this is the point at which Theory Y begins to appear unrealistic. It collides head on with pervasive attitudes associated with management by direction and control.

The assumptions of Theory Y imply that unless integration is achieved the organization will suffer. The objectives of the organization are not achieved best by the unilateral administration of promotions, because this form of management by direction and control will not create the commitment that would make available the full resources of those affected. The lesser motivation, the lesser resulting degree of self-direction and self-control are costs that when added up for many instances over time, will more than offset the gains obtained by unilateral decisions "for the good of the organization."

RENSIS LIKERT, THE TECHNICIAN, AND THE CONCEPT OF MEASUREMENT

Rensis Likert built on the results of the earlier Hawthorne research and on McGregor's Theory Y principles in order to describe a systematic approach to participative management called System IV. He conducted research that showed the System IV participative management approach to be superior to other management approaches in the results obtained, as measured by such objective criteria as productivity, profitability, turnover, and employee satisfaction. He stressed the need for a corporate-wide culture of cooperation and demonstrated that there is a statistically significant correlation between employee attitudes and objective criteria of performance.

In Likert's System IV organization:

1. Management has complete confidence and trust in subordinates.
2. Decision making is widely dispersed and decentralized.

3. Employees are motivated by participation and involvement in decision making.
4. There is extensive, friendly superior-subordinate interaction.
5. There is widespread responsibility for control, with all employees fully involved.

Perhaps Likert's greatest contribution, however, was pioneering the development of a measurement technique for accurately evaluating organizational culture and employee attitudes. Moreover, Likert was the first to apply measurement on a wide scale and continuing basis as a routine management tool. This work of Likert, in developing a questionnaire technique for evaluating organizational culture and employee attitudes, provided the groundwork for the development of the *Human Resources Index* that is discussed in this book.

Likert describes his System IV participative management as follows:[4]

The supervisors and managers in American industry and government who are achieving the highest productivity, lower costs, least turnover and absence, and the highest levels of employee motivation and satisfaction display, on the average, a different pattern of leadership from those managers who are achieving less impressive results. The principles and practices of these high-producing managers are deviating in important ways from those called for by present-day management theories.

The high-producing managers whose deviations from existing theory and practice are creating improved procedures have not yet integrated their deviant principles into a theory of management. Individually, they are often clearly aware of how a particular practice of theirs differs from generally accepted methods, but the magnitude, importance, and systematic nature of the differences when the total pattern is examined do not appear to be recognized.

Based upon the principles and practices of the managers who are achieving the best results, a newer theory of organization and management can be stated. An attempt will be made . . . to present briefly some of the overall characteristics of such a theory and to formulate a general integrating principle which can be useful in attempts to apply it.

Research findings indicate that the general pattern of operations of the highest-producing managers tends to differ from that of the managers of mediocre and low-producing units by more often showing the following characteristics:

1. A preponderance of favorable attitudes on the part of each member of the organization toward all the other members, toward superiors, toward the work, toward the organization—toward all aspects of the job. These favorable attitudes toward others reflect a high level of

mutual confidence and trust throughout the organization. The favorable attitudes toward the organization and the work are not those of easy complacency, but are the attitudes of identification with the organization and its objectives and a high sense of involvement in achieving them. As a consequence, the performance goals are high and dissatisfaction may occur whenever achievement falls short of the goals set.

2. The organization consists of a tightly knit, effectively functioning social system. This social system is made up of the interlocking work groups with a high degree of group loyalty among the members and favorable attitudes and trust between superiors and subordinates. Sensitivity to others and relatively high levels of skill in personal interaction and the functioning of groups are also present. These skills permit effective participation in decisions on common problems. Participation is used, for example, to establish organizational objectives which are a satisfactory integration of the needs and desires of all members of the organization and of persons functionally related to it. High levels of reciprocal influence occur, and high levels of total coordinated influence are achieved in the organization. Communication is efficient and effective. There is a flow from one part of the organization to another of all the relevant information important for each decision and action. The leadership in the organization has developed what might well be called a highly effective social system for interaction and mutual influence.

3. Measurements of organizational performance are used primarily for self guidance rather than for superimposed control. To tap the motives which bring cooperative and favorable rather than hostile attitudes, participation and involvement in decisions is a habitual part of the leadership processes. This kind of decision-making, of course, calls for the full sharing of available measurements and information. Moreover, as it becomes evident in the decision-making process that additional information or measurements are needed, steps are taken to obtain them. . . .

Widespread use of participation is one of the more important approaches employed by the high-producing managers in their efforts to get full benefit from the technical resources of the classical theories of management coupled with high levels of reinforcing motivation. This use of participation applies to all aspects of the job and work, as, for example, in setting work goals and budgets, controlling costs, organizing the work. . . .

In these and comparable ways, the high-producing managers make full use of the technical resources of the classical theories of management. They use these resources in such a manner, however, that favorable and cooperative attitudes are created and all members of the organization endeavor to pull concertedly toward commonly accepted goals which they have helped to establish. . . .

How do these high-producing managers build organizations which display this central characteristic? Is there any general approach or underlying principle which they rely upon in building highly motivated organizations? There seems to be, and clues as to the nature of the principle can be obtained by reexamining some of the (previous) material. . . . The research findings show, for example, that those supervisors and managers whose pattern of leadership yields consistently favorable attitudes more often think of employees as "human beings rather than just as persons to get the work done." Consistently, in study after study, the data show that treating people as "human beings" rather than as "cogs in a machine" is a variable highly related to the attitudes and motivation of the subordinates at every level in the organization. . . .

The superiors who have the most favorable and cooperative attitudes in their work groups display the following characteristics. The attitude and behavior of the superior toward the subordinate as a person, as *perceived by the subordinate,* is as follows:

> He is supportive, friendly, and helpful rather than hostile. He is kind but firm, never threatening, genuinely interested in the well-being of subordinates, and endeavors to treat people in a sensitive, considerate way. He is just, if not generous. He endeavors to serve the best interests of his employees as well as of the company.
>
> He shows confidence in the integrity, ability, and motivations of subordinates rather than suspicion and distrust.
>
> His confidence in subordinates, leads him to have high expectations as to their level of performance. With confidence that he will not be disappointed, he expects much, not little. (This, again, is fundamentally a supportive rather than a critical or hostile relationship.) . . .
>
> The leader develops his subordinates into a working team with high group loyalty by using participation and other kinds of group-leadership practices summarized (earlier).

CHRIS ARGYRIS, THE MANAGEMENT CRITIC, AND SHORTCOMINGS OF TRADITIONAL STRATEGIES

Chris Argyris believes that there is a fundamental contradiction between the basic needs of the individual and the demands of the typical organization. Traditional hierarchical organizations, Argyris says, require highly specialized jobs that result in boring and alienating work. While he believes there is a fundamental inconsistency between the needs of individuals and the demands of traditional organizations, he points out that organizations built upon a culture of trust in employees can facilitate widespread participation in planning and decision making, and permit the design of more complex jobs requiring greater individual autonomy and responsibility. In other words, organizational systems that are designed to pay more attention to employees' needs can be much more productive, which is the underlying rationale of Strategy A.

Argyris summarized his theory as follows:[5]

Bringing together the evidence regarding the impact of the formal organizational principles upon the individual, it is concluded that there are some basic incongruencies between the growth trends of a healthy personality and the requirements of the formal organization. If the principles of formal organization are used as ideally defined, employees will tend to work in an environment where (1) they are provided minimal control over their workaday world, (2) they are expected to be passive, dependent, and subordinate, (3) they are expected to have a short time perspective, (4) they are induced to perfect and value the frequent use of a few skin surface shallow abilities, and (5) they are expected to produce under conditions leading to psychological failure.

All these characteristics are incongruent to the ones *healthy* human beings are postulated to desire. They are much more congruent with the needs of infants in our culture. In effect, therefore, organizations are willing to pay high wages and provide adequate security if mature adults will, for eight hours a day, behave in a less than mature manner! *If the analysis is correct, this inevitable incongruency increases (1) as the employees are of increasing maturity, (2) as the formal structure (based upon the above principles) is made more clear-cut and logically tight for maximum formal organizational effectiveness, (3) as one goes down the line of command, and (4) as the jobs become more and more mechanized (i.e., take on assembly line characteristics).*

Further indirect evidence is provided by Arensberg, who "revisited" the famous Hawthorne Studies. He noted that many of the results reported about the relay assembly experiments occurred after the (women) were placed in a work situation where they were (1) made "subjects" of an "important" experiment, (2) encouraged to participate in decisions affecting their work, (3) given veto power over supervisors to the point where, as they testify, "we have no boss." Clearly these conditions constitute a sweeping shift in the basic relationship of modern industrial work where the employee is subordinate to people above him.

FROM HAWTHORNE TO STRATEGY A

These then are the major management theorists whose work provided the rationale for the innovative approach discussed in this book. Their work also underlies what we have come to think of as the characteristic Japanese style of management—attention to the needs of employees, emphasis on participation, decision making through consensus, massive effort to facilitate communication at all levels, breaking down status barriers and other barriers to communication, and the development of a work culture that emphasizes the integration of individual goals and organizational objectives. This latter step consists of creating organizational cultures in which individuals truly believe that they can achieve their own personal goals *best* by participating in a joint effort to achieve widely shared organizational values and objectives.

These same theorists provide the underpinning for Strategy A, a process for moving an organization away from an authoritarian, bureaucratic culture and toward a participative culture that attempts to integrate the goals of individuals with the goals of the organization in order to achieve high levels of productivity.

The core idea that ties together Strategy A with the work of Homans, McGregor, Likert, and Argyris, and which also characterizes the Japanese style of management, is the theme of obtaining employee *commitment* to the goals of the organization. In an era in which organizations frequently confront the necessity of massive change, committed employees can be an extremely valuable organizational resource in facilitating rapid adaptation to changing conditions. This is why many firms such as Delta Air Lines, Toyota Motor Manufacturing (USA), Saturn, and Federal Express have thrived by knowing that under conditions of rapid change committed employees were their most important competitive edge. As the vice president of human resources at Toyota Motor Manufacturing in Georgetown, Kentucky, has put it:[6]

People are behind our success. Machines don't have new ideas, solve problems, or grasp opportunities. Only people who are involved and thinking can make a difference ... every auto plant in the U.S. has basically the same machinery. But how people are utilized and involved varies widely from one company to another. The work force gives any company its true competitive edge.

NOTES

1. George C. Homans, *Fatigue of Workers* (New York: Reinhold Publishing Corporation, 1941), pp. 56–65.
2. Douglas McGregor, *The Human Side of Enterprise* (New York: McGraw-Hill Book Co., Inc., 1960), chap. 3, pp. 33–42.

3. Douglas McGregor, *The Human Side of Enterprise* (New York: McGraw-Hill Book Co., Inc., 1960), chap. 4, pp. 45–52.
4. Rensis Likert, *New Patterns of Management* (New York: McGraw-Hill Book Co., Inc., 1961), chap. 8, pp. 97–101.
5. Chris Argyris, *Personality and Organization* (New York: Harper & Row Publishers, 1957), pp. 66–69.
6. Gary Dessler, *Human Resource Management,* 6th ed. (Englewood Cliffs, NJ: Prentice-Hall, 1994), p. 18.

4 PATTERNS FOR SUCCESS: COMPANIES THAT UTILIZE MAJOR PORTIONS OF STRATEGY A

Over the last few years, a number of companies have been discovering assets that do not appear on the balance sheet and which often go unrecognized by top management. These hidden assets are the company's human resources.

How is it possible for valuable resources to be unrecognized? Simply because many managers have grown accustomed to thinking of the workforce as a necessary cost of production rather than a company asset—one that represents a sizable investment. Many companies that take the trouble to add up their total investment in the human organization (including costs of recruitment, selection, training, and development) are shocked to discover that it is greater than their investment in physical assets.

Some companies making this discovery have come to the conclusion that such valuable resources need to be managed and utilized at least as carefully as the company's physical plant. They have started searching for better ways to utilize these newly recognized assets and to realize their full potential.

Relatively few companies have truly begun to think of (and to manage) their human resources as though they were an investment, and only a handful of these companies have been at it long enough for the results to be clear. Evidence is beginning to mount, however, that the payoff from this approach can be well worth the effort and cost. Firms pioneering in the use of this approach, such as Hewlett-Packard, IBM,

Motorola, Delta Air Lines, Walt Disney, Donnelly Mirrors (Donnelly Corporation), Lincoln Electric, and Harman-International, have already demonstrated that careful attention to employees can have tangible bottom-line results appreciated by stockholders.

Because major management changes can more easily be introduced in smaller organizations, some small companies are also achieving outstanding results. Increases in individual productivity of 50 percent are not uncommon when companies begin to utilize their human resources effectively and harness the hitherto untapped potential for commitment to the goals of the organization.

The approaches for doing this come primarily from the results of behavioral science research that has shown that many employees—perhaps most—in the typical organization contribute less than 50 percent of what they potentially could contribute to the success of the organization. The research also indicates that much of this potential contribution is lost for reasons beyond the control of the individual employee, but well within the control of top management. Most of this lost contribution of effort can be traced to undermotivation of the workforce.

On the other hand, we have also learned that motivation is *not* something that can be done *to* or *for* somebody. Motivation, involvement, and commitment to organization goals can come only from *within the individual.* What management can do is create the conditions that make it possible for individuals to commit, to involve, and to motivate themselves. All too often, these conditions are lacking.

More and more executives are realizing that most people are naturally innovative and want to work hard; however, they often don't because management doesn't create the kind of environment in which they can. Employees always want to be involved—the problem is lack of management involvement.

A workable participatory management program requires a change in attitude throughout an organization, and that change must be supported from the top. Too many participatory experiments start off well, only to fail because they represented a deviant subculture in a company whose dominant culture is authoritarian.

EVIDENCE OF THE CONNECTION BETWEEN EMPLOYEE-CENTERED MANAGEMENT AND PERFORMANCE

Among the firms that have been the subject of careful study to document the use of attention to employees as a major corporate strategy leading to superior financial performance are Hewlett-Packard, Donnelly Mirrors Company (Donnelly Corporation), Walt Disney, IBM, Southwest Airlines, and Harman-International Industries.

Donnelly Mirrors Company (Donnelly Corporation) is best known for its emphasis on participative management and its productivity bonus plan for providing employees a monthly bonus directly tied to improvements in productivity. There are two unusual features of this plan:

1. It is a *group* bonus in which *every* employee in the company receives the same *percentage* increase in base salary.
2. The size of the bonus is tied directly to improvements in *productivity*, not profits.

Although less well known, one of the steps which John Donnelly, the company president, took to implement the philosophy of employee-centered management was the regular use of employee attitude surveys. In fact, in earlier years Rensis Likert served as a consultant to Donnelly Mirrors (Donnelly Corporation), using employee attitude surveys as an organization change mechanism for introducing System IV management.

Harman-International Industries (manufacturers of Harman-Kardon and JBL high fidelity equipment) gained national attention when the company placed some highly unusual full-page ads in the *Wall Street Journal* and *New York Times* announcing in bold headlines "Concern for the Development of Our People is the Primary Cause of Significant Improvement in Sales, Earnings, and Return on Investment." Harman-International experienced within a span of five years a phenomenal growth in revenues from $43 million to over $136.5 million and, perhaps even more remarkably, *simultaneously* posted an increase in return on investment from 22 percent to 30.1 percent. It will be obvious to readers that this is, at the very least, an extremely rare financial performance for a *Fortune* 1000 corporation.

While a technically excellent product and sound financial and marketing management are also important components of this firm's strategy, it is fascinating that the chairman and president, Dr. Sidney Harman, says that the *primary cause* of financial success has been the company's attention to employee needs and motivation. He says, "Workers are active participants in the significant decisions that affect their working lives," including participation in "planning the quotations and making the necessary commitments" to submit bids for new work. "It is our growing conviction and our growing purpose to make work at every level interesting and properly responsive to the needs of all our people. Our experience . . . vividly demonstrates the compatibility between such an approach, and growth and success in the more traditional business terms."

Although Hewlett-Packard, Donnelly Mirrors (Donnelly Corporation), IBM, Walt Disney, Southwest Airlines, and Harman-International are in very different industries and face radically different competitive environments, a pattern of striking similarities emerges when they are compared. Among the characteristics they share are:

- A strong, influential leader as CEO during the early formative period of the organization who infused the corporate culture with bone-deep beliefs in the dignity and value of the individual employee; the company culture and management philosophy reflect the personal beliefs of this influential individual.
- A fundamental commitment (springing from the corporate culture) to a policy that emphasizes attention to employees as a major corporate strategy for achieving high performance and profitability.
- An unusually loyal and committed workforce with high levels of morale and motivation as objectively measured by *employee attitude surveys,* which the management tends to utilize as a *routine management tool.*
- Extremely low rates of absenteeism and turnover.
- Consistently outstanding organizational performance over an extended period of time, as measured by both market dominance in their industry and exceptional financial performance.
- A common pattern of corporate history in which the corporate culture, emphasizing the dignity of individuals and the strategy of "attention to employees," clearly precedes by many years the outstanding financial performance. In other words, it is clear that the outstanding financial performance did not come first and make it possible to adopt such a strategy as merely a "luxury" in an affluent organization.
- Finally, and most significantly, each of these organizations is headed by an individual who *attributes* the outstanding performance of the organization in large part to the emphasis on attention to employees.

In addition to the preceding organizations, we are all aware of the surprising success that Japanese firms such as Toyota, Honda, Sony, and Nissan seem to be having in America. In these plants, Japanese executives are achieving productivity and quality records with American workers that surpass those of traditional American plants. Although technically skilled in many areas of management, the Japanese themselves consistently say that their biggest competitive advantage is the closeness and cooperation between executives and employees, achieved through such practices as de-emphasis of status differences (standard uniforms, no executive dining rooms, private offices, or reserved parking), emphasis on communication, and attention to employee needs.

OPINION SURVEYS AT IBM[1]

The first opinion survey was taken within IBM 40 years ago. Since its experimental beginning at IBM Poughkeepsie in 1957, the opinion survey program has grown in importance as a way for employees, protected by anonymity, to tell management of their concerns and to discuss corrective action at follow-up or "feedback" meetings with their colleagues and managers. In short, the program not only takes regular temperature readings of employee satisfaction, but if a touch of fever is detected, it also permits the patient to help with the cure.

The dips and rises of employee satisfaction are monitored by division and location, and a morale index of the company, worldwide, is examined in detail by the Corporate Management Committee at Armonk at least twice a year. Every 18 months or so, employees are asked a number of the same questions as to how they feel about their job, career, compensation, management, company, and overall satisfaction, because these are among the "corporate core" items on which the index is based. If the questions didn't remain the same, there could be no basis for comparison.

One measurement of employee confidence in the program is the extent of participation (always voluntary), which averages about 85 percent worldwide.

In its 40 years of use at IBM, the employee opinion survey has earned respect and credibility, not only as a management tool, but as an important way for employees to let off steam and contribute remedies to departmental problems. "Certainly, the corporation doesn't manage its people solely by opinion surveys and numbers on an index," says W. E. Burdick. "There are many ways for employees to make known their dissatisfaction. But the survey program offers them the chance to work with their managers to change what has to be changed." A key divisional executive has commented:

Some of our people are disinclined to complain. Yet we want to know what's on their minds. The survey questionnaire is their opportunity to express opinions candidly and with anonymity. I find the survey results valuable because they enable every level of management in the division to assess areas of strength and weakness and what must be improved. Also, comparing the results with those of previous surveys helps measure the effectiveness of earlier remedial action by management. The greatest pay-off is when managers review the survey results with employees and work with them on what, if anything, ought to be done. Life being what it is, the next survey will still show problems, but if the system is working, they won't all be the same ones. That's progress.[2]

There is other business justification for such concern with employee attitudes. An early relation was found between productivity and employee satisfaction. People with better morale on the job tended to be absent less often, to visit the infirmary less frequently, and to be more consistently and reliably productive.

It was also found that feedback meetings sharply increased employee belief that the survey information would be used by management to change things. In one location, 84 percent of those who had received no feedback said they doubted that the survey results would be used. But of those who had been told the results, only 11 percent regarded the surveys as a futile exercise. Today, all employees routinely participate in such meetings.

Managers have considerable flexibility in developing survey data. Functional managers are encouraged to submit questions tailored to their areas. Tailoring questions to local issues is common practice.

The survey administrator has all written comments typed up before review, and the written versions destroyed. The company wants confidentiality as much as the employee does because it is the key to obtaining truthful answers.

DONNELLY CORPORATION[3]

Another firm that has achieved outstanding financial performance through a strategy emphasizing attention to employees is Donnelly Corporation, which manufactures automotive mirror, window, interior lighting, and trim systems.

The distinctive management culture of Donnelly Corporation can be traced directly back to the personal philosophy of John Donnelly. Although Mr. Donnelly was educated as an engineer at Notre Dame, he then entered a seminary to prepare for the priesthood. After his father died in 1932, Donnelly was called out of the seminary to help manage the company, which had been family owned since its founding in 1905. Except for one brief return to the seminary, John Donnelly headed the company until his death in 1986.

Donnelly, who had studied the writings of both Douglas McGregor and Rensis Likert, was a strong believer in participative management; this is the key philosophy that defines the culture of Donnelly Corporation. John Donnelly has said: "If you pay attention to people, they perform better. At Western Electric Company during the famous Hawthorne experiment, researchers found that even if you turn off the lights, employees performed better. And what we're trying to do is pay attention to people on a constant basis. So, in a way, what we're trying to do is to have a continuous Hawthorne effect."

On another occasion, Donnelly related the following incident:

After one industrial engineer had been in the company for about a month, I happened to see him and he said, "This is absolutely unbelievable." I said, "What do you mean?" He said, "Well, I go around and talk to people about problems that I see and they are willing to let me have the information without any fuss about it." "Do you know why that is?" I asked. "Well, I suppose it has something to do with the system," he said. "They expect that you are not going to abuse the information and that if you want to do something with it you will talk it over with them and that if there are problems because of it, you'll work it out together." "That's true—we do give out information that is not usually given out, and we trust employees to use it properly. So people can see a difference here. They like the difference, but they may not know how to foster it. They may think it's a magic formula and that you don't have to keep working at it."

Among the many things that have been done to promote a team spirit at Donnelly Corporation and to put all employees on an equal basis in order to foster participation have been eliminating time clocks and putting all people on salary. Donnelly Corporation has also implemented a Scanlon Plan under which all employees, from the president down to the newest sweeper, participate equally in a monthly productivity bonus fund—which is the result of cost savings generated by improving productive efficiency. In the Donnelly version of the Scanlon Plan, any improvement in actual cost of production, as compared to standard cost, generates a savings pool equal to the dollar value of the cost savings. This pool is then split between the shareholders and employees. All employees, regardless of organizational level and seniority, receive the same percentage of their base salary as a monthly productivity bonus.

According to John Donnelly, however, the financial bonus is not the primary motivator; it merely serves as the equitable distribution to employees of their share of the benefits generated by their cooperative efforts. The primary motivation, Donnelly believes, is the opportunity to participate in work teams that meet on company time to generate ideas for productivity improvement, and to review the ideas submitted by other employees throughout the company. Everyone is invited and urged to submit suggestions for productivity improvements, not only in his or her own job and work operation, but in any job throughout the company, including the president's office. Because everyone in the company shares proportionately in the benefits of any productivity savings, there is a tremendous incentive to both produce savings oneself and cooperate with others to make cost-saving efforts succeed instead of resisting or inventing obstacles. As a result of this organizational climate, employees frequently suggest ways to eliminate jobs in production, supervision, and other activities. Comments John Donnelly:

Here's the sort of thing that happens: A team of five people was feeding and unloading a multi-stage injection molding machine. By their own decision, they modified the work so that four could keep the machine loaded. Since there were two machines operating three shifts, six jobs were eliminated. The holders of those jobs, though, were guaranteed a continuation of their wages for six months. All were placed in new jobs before the end of the six-month period.

Of course, an essential element in making people willing to suggest ways to eliminate jobs is that Donnelly works very hard to provide job security for employees. If a job is eliminated through productivity improvements, instead of laying off the individual who holds the job, he or she is retrained for another job.

One unique feature of the Donnelly Scanlon Plan is that the Plan formula is *not* adjusted to reflect the effects of new equipment. This practice reflects John Donnelly's philosophy of trust in the individual employee and confidence in the ability of employees at all levels to participate meaningfully in generating productivity savings through cooperative effort. John Donnelly explains:

Once again, we departed from the usual approach. Usually companies using the Scanlon Plan have tried to separate the improvements made by new machines from the improvements made by workers. Since the operators had not contributed to buying the machine, management reasoned it should change the base of the bonus. But we didn't like that philosophy. We wanted both the workers and the company to share in the savings. To us it seemed logical *not* to change the bonus base.

Two other reasons supported our conclusion. First, we found it helpful to involve the operators in the selection or design of equipment because they had very practical ideas which we could not afford to overlook. Thus, many people were contributing to the purchase of the machine—operators, engineers, and buyers. Also, we wanted these machines to produce up to or over their stated capacity. Too often, it seems to me, business finds that labor-saving devices create feather-bedding, so that the devices fail to achieve their potential savings. By not factoring the machine improvement out of the bonus base, we made it possible for our people to receive better equipment and have a stake in getting maximum results from it.

A Donnelly employee typically works in a team of 15 people. Each employee is trusted to keep his or her own records but is responsible to other members of the team. If someone is late to work because of car trouble or an illness in the family, his or her work will be covered by another team member. Each team member has a primary job, but is expected to be able to do the jobs done by other members on the team. Thus, if one team member is frequently absent or not performing well during working hours, he or she has to answer not just to the company but to the other team members. Informal social pressure is a very important part of the control mechanism at Donnelly. Each team also sets its own production goals, within the framework of company-wide objectives, and team members meet together as a group to decide what their salaries should be in relation to some overall guidelines established by the company.

Employees at Donnelly are given a great deal of information about the management and financial condition of the organization. Information on the level of business obtained, costs, and profitability is regularly distributed to employees in company newsletters and discussed at frequent meetings. At Donnelly, all such financial matters are presented openly both at meetings and in the company newspaper.

John Donnelly credits the regular use of employee attitude surveys as being a key management practice in carrying out the philosophy of participative management. He says: "We began conducting regular surveys of employee attitudes, with special emphasis on employees' relations with teams—another of Rensis Likert's ideas."

The step that attracted most attention, perhaps, began with a proposal at one of the work team meetings. The proposal was to eliminate time clocks and put all people on salary. After this idea had been debated at length in work team meetings, it was put to an employee vote, and it was voted in.

Although some of Donnelly's management practices may seem radical to executives in more traditional organizational cultures, the best measure of their effectiveness is simply to examine their effect on the bottom line. As stated by Robert Levering, et al., in _The 100 Best Companies to Work For In America,_ "Executives from other companies (and from other countries) trek regularly to Holland, Michigan, to learn how Donnelly Mirrors [Donnelly Corporation] does it. Most people are surprised to learn that Donnelly makes 98 percent of the rear-view mirrors found in American-made automobiles."

Thirty years ago, Donnelly Mirrors (Donnelly Corporation) had several competitors, but these have literally been driven out of the market by Donnelly's ability to hold down prices through continuous productivity improvements and cost savings. Moreover, Donnelly is a highly profitable organization.

John Donnelly was asked in an interview by the _Harvard Business Review_ why other companies do not adopt his ideas. He replied: "They're afraid of losing authority. Organizations are mostly modeled after the military, and it's difficult for people to conceive of any other system working. I would be the last one to say that we don't use authority in this company. We do. But, to the extent that you have to rely on the authority of your position, you're a questionable manager. If you are not in the position to get people to accept ideas because they're sound, and if you are not willing to accept an idea because it's sound, then you're really not a good manager."

John Donnelly prominently displayed over his desk a sign which read: "People are important," and he once commented, "As a businessman I can see that traditional management is just a damn inefficient way to operate. American industry is losing its trading position in the world because of its failure to allow people to be human or mature or adult in their work situations."

In keeping with this philosophy, in addition to the suggestion-screening committee that was established as part of the Scanlon Plan to discuss and approve productivity improvement suggestions, a second structure called the Employees' Committee was added to encourage participation in decision making for other issues. This committee is made up of employee representatives, and its purpose is to "facilitate the resolution of issues of fairness not immediately related to production but having consequences for most employees." This aspect of the organization is called the "equity structure" by the company, and it is intended to differentiate participation on issues of equity from participation on issues related to task achievement.

A manager of human resources for Donnelly Corporation has commented as follows in summarizing the company's experience with participative management:

The Scanlon Plan has made a significant contribution to our successful development over the years. We adopted this plan in 1952 and since then we have grown to appreciate why the behavioral scientist, Douglas McGregor, described it as a "way of life." Yes, it has truly prescribed a way of life for us at Donnelly for over forty years, a way of life which has continuously emphasized human potential and encouraged us to search for creative ways in which this potential could be more fully realized.

Over the years many attitude surveys have been conducted at Donnelly, involving all employees. A key executive has commented that these surveys:

provided valuable information about our organization culture, and the thorough feedback process following each survey led to significant change. . . . In effect, we changed from a task structure based on representation to a task structure where every employee as a member of a work team could directly participate in decisions affecting his/her work. This is the task structure through which we serve our customers today. Every Donnelly employee is a member of at least one work team. We depend on these work teams to generate cost reductions on a continuous basis. We encourage teams to meet regularly to set goals, discuss variances, and solve problems.

A fairly recent change in the financial bonus system of Donnelly has been the addition of a new profit-sharing bonus. The basic productivity-sharing bonus based on productivity improvements has been maintained, but to it has now been added an additional profit-sharing bonus in which all employees participate. Under this new profit-sharing formula, after a 5¼ percent return on investment has been set aside for shareholders, the remaining profits are divided between employees and the shareholders, with the employees receiving 44 percent and the shareholders receiving 56 percent.

NOTES

1. Some of the material in this section is adapted from *THINK: The IBM Magazine.*
2. Ibid., Nov./Dec., 1982.
3. The comments of John F. Donnelly reported in this section are reprinted by permission of the *Harvard Business Review* ("Participative Management at Work," *Harvard Business Review,* January/February, 1977).

5 STRATEGY A APPLIED: BREAKTHROUGH IN ORGANIZATION PERFORMANCE

This chapter describes the experience over a six-year period of a Canadian firm that implemented Strategy A, a structured seven-step strategy for improved organization performance through employee-centered management. A significant change in the condition of the human organization resulting from the intervention was documented over the six-year period and was shown to be correlated with a 66 percent increase in profitability. The results of the study indicate that in the Canadian/U.S. context, sustainable competitive advantage can be achieved in some instances through employee-centered management that encourages widespread participation and contribution of employees in problem solving and decision making.

A dramatic breakthrough in organization performance took place at Ault Foods, Ltd., of Canada as the result of implementing Strategy A. The process used for organization change is a generic strategy that would be appropriate for a wide range of organizations in North America. Thus, the pattern of performance improvement described here can be replicated by many organizations. The survey instrument used in this intervention to implement employee-centered management is the *Human Resources Index.*

THE *HUMAN RESOURCES INDEX (HRI)*

The *HRI* is a standardized employee survey instrument that measures employee perceptions of 15 key variables identified with organizational performance. It is useful in identifying opportunities for improvement of the human organization and in implementing changes to enhance competitiveness.

Because survey results indicate an organization's strengths and weaknesses, a standardized survey provides the advantage of comparing results against norms established by data from other organizations as well as against internal norms in other departments. In addition to their measurement function, surveys may also be used to facilitate planned organization change and team-building based on feedback and discussion of the survey data.

The *Human Resources Index* contains 64 positive statements about the organization, for which each employee is asked to indicate her or his level of agreement using a five-point scale. The last two items in the instrument provide an open-ended opportunity to indicate things that are "most liked" about the organization and things the employee would "most like to change." There is also an opportunity for each firm to add custom items to the standardized instrument in order to assess unique or particular issues or conditions.

The 64 items are scored and reported individually; more importantly, they are also used to determine a composite score on each of the following 15 factors:

1. Reward system
2. Communication
3. Organization effectiveness
4. Concern for people
5. Organizational objectives
6. Cooperation
7. Intrinsic satisfaction
8. Structure
9. Relationships
10. Climate
11. Participation
12. Work group
13. Intergroup competence
14. First-level supervision
15. Quality of management

The scores on the 15 factors become the initial focus in analyzing and comparing results from one organization with another or in comparing changes over time within a single organization. Once critical factors are identified, the scores on individual items become very important in pinpointing the cause of a particular attitude and in understanding its significance.

The *HRI* has been used in firms representing a wide range of industries and sizes, and norms have been developed that are proving remarkably stable. A primary focus of further research with the instrument at this point is on investigating separate norms for different national cultures, separate industry norms, the correlation between changes in the *HRI* and changes in operating data, and the lag time between significant changes in *HRI* data and significant changes in operating data.

Perhaps the most important conclusion that can be reached from the work that has been done is that this approach is quite practical as a means for benchmarking the strategic management of an organization's human resources. Moreover, the survey data have proved highly useful in diagnosing specific problems requiring concentrated attention and in initiating organization development by opening up two-way communication about matters of practical significance to the organization.

Derivation of Factors and Psychometric Qualities of the *HRI*

Both the factors and the individual items were initially generated a priori. Subsequently, individual items and factors were refined through a process of review by a panel of experts in survey design and a panel of personnel managers participating in a pilot study of the instrument.

The current factors were determined by factor analysis of the data from over 12,000 respondents representing a broad cross section of organizations. More than 50 private and public sector organizations are represented in the current norm pool, which includes electronics manufacturing, retail, banking, professional, research and development, agricultural, hospitality, health care, consumer goods manufacturing, resort operations, and governmental organizations. The sizes of the included groups range from 50 to 4000.

The reliability of the overall instrument and of the individual factors was determined using Cronbach's Alpha, a statistic widely accepted as a general purpose measure of reliability. The alpha coefficients calculated for the total instrument and for the individual factors are shown in Exhibit 5-1. The reliabilities ranging from 0.757 to 0.929 were judged to be more than satisfactory to justify further use of the instrument.

Exhibit 5-1 *Coefficient Alpha Reliabilities*

Scale	Alpha Coefficient
Total Instrument	0.978
Factors:	
Reward system	0.774
Communication	0.894
Organization effectiveness	0.901
Concern for people	0.828
Organizational objectives	0.874
Cooperation	0.852
Intrinsic satisfaction	0.888
Structure	0.757
Relationships	0.765
Climate	0.929
Participation	0.852
Work group	0.766
Intergroup competence	0.799
Quality of management	0.866

The validity of the instrument was determined through a process of content validation. Since no equivalent instrument with previously validated factors was known to exist, it was not possible to determine predictive validity through correlation with a criterion measure. Moreover, content validation seems the more reasonable approach for an instrument consisting of items directly reporting individuals' perceptions and attitudes. There are two expert judgments involved in the process of content validation: (a) the extent to which each item in a trait or factor scale pertains to the factor as it is defined, and (b) the extent to which the entire set of items represents all aspects of the factor. Each of the factors of the *HRI* was judged to be "highly valid" by a panel of human resource managers.

THE AULT FOODS INTERVENTION

The subject firm for this implementation study, Ault Foods, Ltd., is a diversified dairy products processing and marketing firm of about 3000 employees widely dispersed in several major regions of Canada. Data collection has been ongoing at Ault Foods since 1988; annual measures of organization culture representing all employees (using the *Human Resources Index*) now exist for six data points.

The data have been collected with breakdowns by division, plant or department, function, level, and gender.

Ault Foods, with Corporate Offices in Toronto, is recognized as one of the leading dairy processors and distributors in North America, with annual sales in excess of $1.4 billion and over 3000 employees. In 1992, Ault was recognized as Dairy Processor of the Year for North America, the first time that a Canadian organization was recognized as the recipient of this prestigious award. Significant technological process and product breakthroughs have occurred in the years following the introduction of a new participative management system.

A corporate strategy was initiated in 1987 to develop and sustain competitive advantage to better compete in the global marketplace; a key element in that strategy was the belief by executive management that sustainable competitive advantage could only be achieved through the participation and contribution of all Ault employees. The new participative management system introduced into the organization was intended to:

- Involve all employees to ensure maximum input and impact on critical business success factors
- Change the way in which the business is managed by making every Ault employee an individual manager of his or her job
- Establish an environment that will encourage employees to express ideas freely and resolve workplace problems quickly and fairly
- Utilize the input of employees who are closest to issues in their identification and resolution
- Empower employees through sharing of decision-making authority

Each employee is a member of a work team in the participative management system, sharing a common vision and reporting relationship. Team leaders are the first-line supervisors, but this role quickly evolves into more of a facilitator/coaching relationship. The workteam system provides the opportunity for team members to provide input into the problem-solving and decision-making processes. Work teams interact on an ad hoc basis with members of other work teams when mutual issues occur or when the services and/or products delivered by one group significantly impact the performance of the other work team.

The other component of the empowerment technology is the fairness/equity system, in which each work team elects a representative to the location Equity Committee. The role of the committee is to monitor the effectiveness of the new management system, resolve issues of fairness/equity submitted by employees after their failure to come to a satisfactory decision with their immediate supervisors, and to provide recommendations on new or modified policies. Each location Equity Committee selects a representative to participate as a member of the Corporate Equity Committee, which meets to address unresolved fairness/equity issues submitted by one of the location Equity Committees and/or new or modified policy recommendations. All decisions made at any level of the fairness/equity system must be by consensus. Any issues that are covered by the terms and conditions of a Collective Bargaining Agreement do not fall within the purview of the Equity Committees.

A key element in implementing employee-centered management at Ault Foods has been use of the *Human Resources Index (HRI)* to track progress of the change process. The integration of the *HRI* into corporate management strategy reflected top management's conviction that employee-centered management could create the ultimate sustainable competitive advantage. The *HRI* has provided benchmarks on key performance indicators, measurement of the effectiveness of human resource interventions, identification of improvement opportunities, and the process by which to involve employees in improving organizational performance. This process is consistent with the principles of the new employee-centered management system, which is seen as a key strategy for developing and sustaining competitive advantage.

Strategy for Implementing Employee-Centered Management

The generic strategy employed at Ault Foods for implementing employee-centered management was Strategy A, described earlier in Chapter 2, which consists of the following seven steps:

1. Determine the baseline condition of the human organization using a validated and standardized survey instrument.
2. Use the survey data to identify and act on key opportunities for improvement worthy of special attention because of a high payout/ investment ratio.
3. Change executive evaluation and reward practices to measure and pay for effective HRM as well as profit, productivity, and costs.

4. Remove artificial barriers to participation, communication, and contribution.
5. Report to employees what has been done to change HRM assumptions and practices, and solicit their participation in planning further change.
6. Measure regularly the condition of the human organization using the same standardized survey instrument to determine changes.
7. Measure the correlation between the *HRI* data and hard criteria of organizational performance—productivity, profitability, growth, costs.

RESULTS OF THE INTERVENTION

The results of the seven-step intervention to implement employee-centered management at Ault Foods are summarized in Exhibit 5-2. The left side of the graph shows the trend line reflecting financial performance of the firm (operating income before nonrecurring expenses) over the five-year period 1983–1987 that immediately preceded the intervention to implement employee-centered management. The right side of the graph tracks progress from 1988–1992 in the overall *HRI* score for the total organization and also shows the trend of operating income over the five-year period 1988–1992 following the intervention. Both the increase in *HRI* score and the increase in operating income from 1988–1992 are statistically significant.

The graph indicates that the trend of operating income has dramatically shifted upward following the implementation of employee-centered management. Operating income of $66.9 million in 1992 represents a 66 percent increase over the average operating income of $40.38 million for the five-year period that preceded the intervention. Moreover, the correlation between yearly *HRI* scores and financial performance over the period 1988–1992 is a surprisingly high 0.866, as indicated in Exhibit 5-3.

While it is impossible to prove causality with absolute certainty, the data strongly support the conclusion that improvement in the motivation, morale, and commitment of the human organization has lead to significantly improved organizational performance, rather than vice versa. Certainly this is the widely held conviction of individuals throughout all echelons of the Ault organization, from top management to the level of operating employees. The fact that the *HRI* scores were typically obtained early in each calendar

Exhibit 5-2 *Operating Income Before and After HRI Intervention*

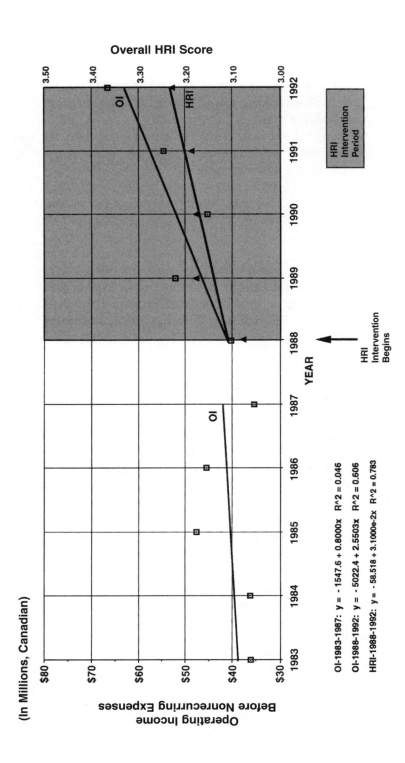

Exhibit 5-3 HRI *Scores and Operating Income*

Year	*HRI* Score	Operating Income ($Canadian)
1983		$36.3M
1984		36.4M
1985		47.8M
1986		45.8M
1987		35.6M
1988	3.08	40.7M
1989	3.18	52.5M
1990	3.18	45.8M
1991	3.19	55.0M
1992	3.23	66.9M

r = 0.866

year and the financial results reflect performance over the entire calendar year adds substantial support to this conclusion regarding the direction of causality. In fact, when the *HRI* survey data were gathered in January or February of each year, performance data for even the *previous* year were not yet known. This time sequence of events virtually rules out the possibility of backward causality (that is, improved performance leads to improved attitudes) in this particular situation.

Moreover, further perspective for interpreting the improvement in performance at Ault Foods over the five-year period is provided by comparing the performance of Ault with the performance of its major competitors. Over the time period 1988–1992 Ault Foods significantly outperformed *each* of its competitors in the Canadian dairy processing industry. The performance of the entire dairy processing industry in Canada was essentially flat over the time period 1988–1992, while Ault Foods was experiencing its dramatic 66 percent increase in operating income. This difference in performance cannot be accounted for by any unique environmental, economic, or competitive factors that affected Ault differentially as compared to the balance of the industry; the only differences were internal management practices.

Specifically, we carefully investigated whether there might have been significant changes in economic, demographic, or product market conditions that affected Ault differentially; or whether company location differences, government regulations, access to markets, or any other differences or changes in the external environment might have somehow favored Ault Foods. Despite careful study of these matters we were unable to discover any external environmental factors that might have accounted for even a small portion of the performance improvement. Moreover, there were no significant internal changes within the organization over the five-year period other than the ones directly related to the intervention to introduce employee-centered management. There were no significant organizational restructurings, changes in employment level, or changes in business strategy (such as product design, product niche, marketing, or process technology) independent of the intervention that might account for the improved performance.

As part of the employee-centered management intervention, however, there was a substantial investment of organizational resources (financial and human) to train both managerial and nonmanagerial personnel in the skills and behaviors required for employee-centered management. Simply stated, although we searched carefully for external environmental conditions or independent strategic changes that might serve as alternative explanations, the only plausible interpretation (which is widely accepted at all levels within the organization) is that the improvement in organizational performance is a direct consequence of the employee-centered management culture.

As a result of its significant improvement in performance, Ault has become widely acknowledged as the industry leader in Canada. In recognition of its performance breakthrough, as stated earlier, Ault was designated by the dairy processing industry as Dairy Processor of the Year for all of North America in 1992.

By squaring the correlation coefficient obtained at Ault Foods between *HRI* scores and operating income ($r = 0.866$) we can ascertain the coefficient of determination, which turns out to be 0.75. This statistic tells us that change in the condition of the human organization accounts for or explains 75 percent of the variation in financial performance (operating income). Though this finding may not be particularly surprising to experienced executives, it is the first time such a clear relationship has actually been documented. Certainly one clear implication of this finding is that interventions to implement employee-centered management have the potential to create dramatic improvement in organization performance. In addition to overall corporate results, the *HRI* scores are broken down each year by specific location, organizational level, job function, gender, and divisional groupings. Customized questions have also been developed for measurement of productivity, equity, communications, and self-management.

BENCHMARKING ORGANIZATIONAL IMPROVEMENT

The following are specific examples of how the *HRI* has been used to benchmark organizational progress and to plan future initiatives for continued improvement:

1. At the beginning of the organization change process in 1987, the Research and Development Group at Ault Foods was targeted as a pilot group for involving a whole function in a planned change effort. Innovation in technology and processing had been identified as a key pillar of the organization's strategic thrust toward improved competitiveness; thus, it was felt that the Research and Development Group had a critical role to play in driving technological improvements throughout the company. However, the group was experiencing difficulties in working together. The employee group would not even meet in the same room with their managers; trust was nonexistent. The *HRI* was used within the Research and Development Group to focus attention on employee involvement and to deal with issues of concern to employees. In the first survey year, the overall *Index* score for the R & D Group was 3.35. A number of issues were identified by employees as problem areas: the weak link between pay and performance, an unsatisfactory compensation program, management's lack of concern for people, absence of a supportive climate, and limited opportunity for participation in decision making. Following a number of changes implemented over the next year regarding rewards, communication, management style, and participation, the overall *Index* score increased the following year to 3.79, a statistically significant change.

   Moreover, it was widely recognized that the work climate had changed dramatically. The survey item concerning a supportive and trusting climate increased from 2.86 to 3.86, a dramatic and statistically significant change. Today the R & D Group is consistently viewed as one of Ault's top performing groups; they have developed many product and process innovations that are key to the organization's financial progress. Moreover, they continue to use the *HRI* data each year to continuously evaluate and improve their own operations and performance.

2. The flagship operation introduced the new employee-centered management system during 1990–1991. On question 48 in the *HRI,* which states "People can participate in and influence decisions

which are important to the operation of their work unit," the 1992
results increased to 3.19 from the 1991 results of 2.98. This statistically significant difference confirms that the new management system has been recognized by the employees at this location as
contributing to their participation in the problem-solving and decision-making processes. The effectiveness of the new management
system at this flagship operation is critical due to its key role in the
success of the organization.

Additional insight into how the *HRI* is being used at Ault Foods
to implement and monitor organization change can perhaps be provided best with an excerpt from the Summary Report of the most
recent administration of the *HRI:*

Perhaps the most significant finding is that 12 locations have shown a
steadily upward trend over the period 1988–1993. For the total Ault organization it is particularly gratifying that the individual factors which have
shown the most improvement are Participation and Communication—both
factors which are directly the focus of Employee-centered Management.
Moreover, of equal importance is the fact that *each* of the 15 factors shows
an increase over the period 1988–1993, and also from last year to this year.
As would be expected and has occurred each year, there is substantial variation among the different locations within the Company.

IMPLICATIONS OF THE
AULT FOODS EXPERIENCE

This study demonstrates that, for many organizations, sustainable
competitive advantage can best be achieved through the participation and contribution of employees in the problem-solving and decision-making processes. Participative approaches will not, however,
fit the circumstances of all organizations. Because the active, wholehearted support of top management is absolutely essential to the
successful implementation of employee-centered management, the
approach described here should not be implemented unless top
management is truly convinced that it represents the *best* opportunity to achieve sustainable competitive advantage.

Nevertheless, in the competitive 1990s, when many organizations
are seeking to achieve significant breakthroughs in operating performance, the seven-step strategy described for implementing employee-
centered management will fit the needs and circumstances of a wide
range of organizations and therefore warrants serious consideration.

Implementing a change strategy requires compelling reasons for change; a participative management process and technology; the identification of critical business success factors to establish benchmarks; an instrument to measure employee perceptions on key factors such as work team effectiveness, organizational effectiveness, intergroup competence, cooperation, and communication; and extensive training.

Part II:
Implementing Strategy A

6   MEASURING THE HUMAN ORGANIZATION: STEP 1 OF STRATEGY A

Since I am proposing that organizations undertake nothing less than a major transformation of their culture and management practice, it is rational for executives to question whether the situation is serious enough to justify such extensive organizational effort. I will respond to this by quoting a shocking statement made by Hajime Karatsu, managing director of Matsushita Communications Industrial Company:

With a few exceptions, U. S. products are of poor quality and not suitable for Japan. Business is not a charity; it follows the laws of supply and demand. Not even Japanese cars, for example, can match the Mercedes-Benz's reputation for elegant comfort. Market forces account for the Mercedes' popularity here and the very few sales of U.S. luxury cars like Cadillacs. Americans need to understand that consumers will not buy products they do not like.[1]

Another indication of what the Japanese think of American management is the following statement by Yoshi Tsurumi, professor of international business at Baruch College, City University of New York:

It is relatively easy to explain the reasons for the decline of one American industry after another in their face-offs against Japanese competitors in the American market. To cite one memorable instance, the Zenith Corp., immediately after gaining protection against Japanese color television imports back in 1977, laid off 5,000 of its American employees and moved its production base to Taiwan. Up until that time, the company had demanded such protection in the name of "saving American jobs."

Over the past two decades, American managers in one industrial sector after another have failed to innovate or improve their company's productivity at the first sign of increased Japanese competition in U.S. markets. Instead, they have preferred to "zap" all of the human resources in sight while salvaging their fixed assets in order to shift production abroad to countries with lower wage costs. This sort of "neutron bomb" mentality on the part of American executives is singularly responsible for the decline of American industry. It was not so much the alleged dumping as the superior quality of individual Japanese firms' color television sets and other products that induced American consumer and industrial customers to switch from American to Japanese products. In the automobile industry, in fact, it was only when Japanese competition forced it to do so that Detroit regained some of its sanity and began to pay attention to quality and customer needs. How else, then, can Japanese conspiracy theorists account for the paradox of the Japanese doing business in the U.S. today? Why, at a time when many American firms are fleeing the U.S. to countries with lower wage scales, are their Japanese counterparts coming into the U.S. to manufacture high quality products using American labor? Many Japanese firms have even taken over and successfully turned around some of the unionized factories in this country that their American competitors had abandoned earlier as uneconomical.[2]

The preceding statements taken together would be infuriating if we did not recognize that they are the simple truth. And the reality is that American workers cannot be given the major blame for America's lack of international competitiveness. The difference is the managerial system. Management, not labor, bears the major responsibility for the decline of American industry. The proof of this statement is found, as stated by Tsurumi, in the many instances in which Japanese firms have taken over American factories in the United States (some of them unionized) that the American firms had simply abandoned as uneconomical, and have successfully turned them around. One of the best examples of this is the Quasar plant in Chicago, which Motorola sold to Japanese interests. Although top management is Japanese, nearly all other employees are Americans, and many of them are the same individuals who operated the plant for Motorola. Under Japanese management a low-quality, money-losing operation has been turned around to produce high-quality products and high profits.

THE LINK BETWEEN CULTURE AND PERFORMANCE

As reported in a *Wall Street Journal* analysis of Japanese management in America, "The Japanese also seem to get more out of their American workers by *paying special attention to them.* . . . Quality doesn't automatically deteriorate when Americans do the job; U.S. auto makers confirm Honda Motor Co.'s assertion that its American-made Accord sedans are equal in quality to Japan-built versions." Robert Crandall, a Brookings Institution economist, says that "many of our failures in the market aren't due to the loss of comparative advantage but to poor management and lethargy."

The traditional bureaucratic/authoritarian style of management (management by direction and control) has failed because it no longer is relevant to the needs of the vast majority of American workers. The time for a major change in management practice has arrived.

Fortunately, this need for change is increasingly being acknowledged by executives and managers. The Conference Board surveyed nearly 1000 senior executives in Conference Board Associate companies to ask their views concerning the top three issues that would be faced by American management over the next few years. Two of the top three issues mentioned by the executives responding were improving productivity and changing the corporate culture. It is clear that most executives see a direct tie between these two issues. The executives indicated that they expect greater productivity to come about primarily through the better use of human resources and the application of new technology. A high percentage of the executives mentioned the following vehicles for improving productivity through better management of people:

- Strengthening the link between pay and performance ("making pay for performance as credible as possible")
- Improving the evaluation of performance (especially managerial and executive performance)
- Incentive pay plans such as executive bonuses and productivity gains-sharing formulas (it is instructive that much more interest was expressed in executive bonuses than in productivity-sharing plans in which all members of the workforce participate as a major strategy for improving productivity)
- Keeping fingers on the pulse of the human organization to measure its present and potential effectiveness

It is not a coincidence that companies seriously committed to obtaining competitive advantage through effective management of people make regular measurement of employee attitudes and perceptions an important element of their management process. Measurement communicates the importance placed by top management on the organization's human resources, and ensures that what is measured will be noticed. One of the most consistent findings of all organizational research is that what is measured gets attention, and what is not measured tends to be ignored. Advanced Micro Devices is one company that regularly measures employee attitudes to make sure that the company strategy of attention to employees is being carried out.

Thus it is clear that a large and growing majority of senior executives in America recognize the need to lead their organizations in a major transition toward a corporate culture that places much more emphasis on attention to employees. The need is recognized; the motivation is present; but the specific vehicle or pattern for such a transition is not nearly so apparent. It is my belief that many executives are seeking a rational, simple, and down-to-earth strategy for initiating and leading such a cultural transformation. This is the role and purpose of Strategy A. As one appliance manufacturing executive has recently put it: "Meaningful involvement of production employees in problem solving will characterize our plant operations for the next several years. Their inputs and our effective attention to them are critical to our success."

The first step in Strategy A is to measure the human organization to assess its condition at the outset of the change process. In order to measure, analyze, and transform the organization's culture, it is necessary to generate information about the quality of organizational performance and about the condition of the organization's human resources. These necessary data include the attitudes, motivation, commitment, and satisfaction level that characterize the human organization. Federal Express, for example, refers to its well-entrenched employee survey-feedback-action program as the "mainstay of its people-first philosophy."

Recent studies indicate quality of work-life issues and the lack of fundamental satisfaction in jobs are major causes of productivity problems. A key executive from a major corporation describes this concern:

I am convinced that the effective management of human resources is going to be critically important in maintaining our profitability as we grow in size and inevitably become somewhat impersonal. Moreover, the effective utilization of human resources can be an important competitive edge for us. With this in mind, I think it's important for us to be able to regularly measure how well we are doing as an organization in managing our human resources and important to be able to track changes over time to identify trouble spots and problems early.

COLLECTING DATA THAT COINCIDE WITH ORGANIZATION OBJECTIVES

Because of this growing attitude, increased attention is being paid to developing tools for analysis and control of the human organization. These tools may be used for measuring the performance of the human resource system, evaluating that performance, and initiating corrective action when it is needed to bring performance in line with organization objectives.

Over the long run, the ultimate criteria for measuring the effectiveness of management are such hard data as return on investment, productivity, absenteeism, turnover, grievance rate, and so on. Because changes in these data may lag behind changes in the condition of the human organization by many months, it is highly useful for management planning and control to supplement these measures with interim measures of the attitudes, motivation, and satisfaction levels of the organization's human resources. A number of leading firms including IBM, Exxon, Xerox, and Motorola are pioneering the development of survey feedback systems that measure the condition of the organization's human resources.

The massive effort that has been underway now for the past 25 years to completely transform the corporate culture of General Motors, using organization development techniques, was initiated by an employee survey conducted by Rensis Likert at the University of Michigan. In this initial study, 5000 workers (both hourly and salaried) in four pilot plants were surveyed to determine their attitudes toward their jobs and the corporation. The study found that employees at all levels felt they had important contributions to make to the management of their plants, and believed they should be given more opportunity to participate. The study also demonstrated a clear relationship between plant performance and employees' attitudes about organizational climate, quality of management, and organizational relationships. As a result of this study, GM decided to split its personnel staff into separate labor relations and personnel staffs. This was designed to allow the director of personnel to be freed from the adversarial role of labor relations, and to concentrate on achieving improved working conditions through cooperation. GM decided to go outside the company and hired Professor Steven H. Fuller of the Harvard Business School as a vice president to head up this new function. In describing the overall organization development effort, Fuller has said: "What we are doing is signaling as obviously and as frequently as we can the commitment of top management that it is interested in improving job satisfaction. We are trying to open the doors and give people an opportunity to share in improving the quality of what they do."

The high regard that Hewlett-Packard employees have for their company has been confirmed by their various climate surveys. In one of the surveys, 7966 employees were interviewed by an outside consulting firm regarding their views on various company practices. The president of the research company reported: "The positive view employees have towards Hewlett-Packard and specifically their feeling of belonging and willingness to recommend the company as a good place to work, places Hewlett-Packard in the upper half of one percent of the more than 1000 U. S. organizations studied in the past quarter century." Other companies that have used employee surveys as a major element of the corporate strategy for creating a highly motivated and committed work force are Motorola, Walt Disney, Procter & Gamble, and General Electric.

As previously discussed, one such survey system for upward communication is called the *Human Resources Index*. The *Index* has been designed to be applicable in a wide range of organizations that wish to:

- Have the advantage of comparing employee responses in their organization with norms determined by the responses of individuals in a broad cross section of other organizations
- Obtain the advantages of the climate survey process without the heavy investment of time and money to develop their own survey instrument internally

THE *HUMAN RESOURCES INDEX (HRI)*

The concept of the *Human Resources Index (HRI)* traces back to the early work on human resource accounting initiated by Rensis Likert in the 1960s. These early efforts attempted to integrate human resource accounting with financial accounting by including human resource valuations on income statements and balance sheets; however, these efforts encountered a number of practical difficulties, including resistance by the accounting profession. As a result, human resource accounting is moving away from the use of financial data and toward the use of climate survey data as the more appropriate measure of the human organization's value and quality.

Because survey results tend to indicate an organization's strengths and weaknesses, it is often helpful to compare results against a standard of norms established for a cross section of other organizations. This is one of the real advantages of using a standardized survey, such as the *HRI*. The *HRI* provides a means for comparing results against norms established by data from other organizations as well as against internal norms established in other departments. Pioneering work in cross-organizational exchange of data has been done by the Mayflower Group, which consists of about 30 companies including IBM, Xerox, General Electric, and Prudential Insurance.

As reported in *Business Week:*

Last year more than 100,000 employees—ranging from production workers to senior managers—minced no words in telling their bosses exactly what they thought of them, the company they work for, and their fellow workers. But instead of being fired, they were encouraged to sound off. Their companies were using a management tool called climate surveys, which not only get employee opinions out in the open but force managers to face up to and correct often unpleasant situations.

Climate surveys can be used both to take the pulse of the organization and to effect change. The *HRI* has proven effective in many organizations for:

- Measuring attitudes, level of satisfaction, and commitment to organizational goals
- Pinpointing specific trouble spots and issues of concern requiring concentrated attention
- Providing a work-related and therefore meaningful basis for opening up real two-way communication and initiating a process of organization development

The first page of the *HRI* is reproduced in Exhibit 6-1 to give an idea of what confronts employees who are asked to participate in a survey. The *Index* contains 64 positive statements about the organization, for

Exhibit 6-1 Human Resources Index

The objective of this survey is to determine how members of this organization feel about the effectiveness with which the organization's human resources are managed. The survey provides you an opportunity to express your opinions in a way that is constructive. Your views will be valuable in assisting the organization to evaluate and improve its performance.

The survey is to be done anonymously. Please **do not put your name** on the response sheet or identify your response in any way. Responses can in no way be traced to any individual. The frank and free expression of your own opinions will be most helpful to the organization.

Listed below are a series of statements. After you have read each statement, please decide the extent to which the statement describes your own situation and your own feelings, using the following scale:

      A) almost never
      B) not often
      C) sometimes (i.e., about half the time)
      D) often
      E) almost always

Then, using a No. 2 pencil darken the appropriate box on the response sheet. For example, if you believe that the statement is true "sometimes" darken block C on the answer sheet next to the number corresponding to the indicated statement.

Questions 65 and 66 should be answered in **pencil** on the back of the **response sheet.**

When you have completed the survey, please return the response sheet and this survey form in accordance with the directions in the cover letter.

IN THIS ORGANIZATION:

1. There is sufficient communication and sharing of information between groups.

2. The skills and abilities of employees are fully and effectively utilized.

3. Objectives of the total organization and my work unit are valid and challenging.

4. The activities of my job are satisfying and rewarding.

5. I have received the amount and kind of training which I need and desire to do my job well.

6. Leadership in this organization is achieved through ability.

7. Rewards are fairly and equitably distributed.

---

*Copyright © , 1977, Fred E. Schuster, Professor of Management, Florida Atlantic University, Boca Raton, Florida.

which the employee is asked to indicate his or her level of agreement. The last two items provide an open-ended opportunity for the respondent to indicate things that are "most liked" about the organization and things he or she would "most like to change."

The 64 items of the *Index* are scored and reported individually; more important, however, they are also used to determine a composite score on each of the following 15 factors:

1. Reward System: compensation, benefits, perquisites, and other (tangible and intangible) rewards
2. Communication: flow of information downward, upward, and across the organization
3. Organization Effectiveness: level of confidence in the overall abilities and success of the organization; how well the organization achieves its objectives
4. Concern for People: degree to which the organization is perceived as caring for its employees
5. Organizational Objectives: extent to which individuals perceive the organization has objectives they can understand, feel proud of, and identify with
6. Cooperation: the ability of people throughout the organization to work effectively together toward shared goals
7. Intrinsic Satisfaction: rewards that people receive from the work itself (sense of achievement, pride in a job well done, growth and development, feeling of competence)
8. Structure: rules and regulations, operating policies and procedures, management practices and systems, the formal organization structure, and reporting relationships
9. Relationships: feelings people have about others in the organization
10. Climate: atmosphere of the organization, the extent to which people see it as a comfortable, supportive, pleasant place to work
11. Participation: opportunity to contribute one's ideas, be consulted, be informed, and play a part in decision making
12. Work Group: feelings about the immediate group of people with whom one works on a daily basis
13. Intergroup Competence: the ability of separate work groups to work smoothly and effectively together to accomplish shared objectives
14. First-Level Supervision: confidence members of the organization have in the competence and integrity of first-line supervisors

15. Quality of Management: confidence that members of the organization have in the competence and integrity of middle and higher management

The scores on the 15 factors become the initial focus in analyzing and comparing results from one organization with another, or in comparing changes over time within a single organization. Once critical factors are identified, the scores on individual items become very important in pinpointing the cause of a particular concern and in understanding its significance for the organization.

Statistical Data Regarding the *Human Resources Index*

For those who are interested in the more technical aspects of the *HRI*, a few comments on its psychometric qualities and on the derivation of the factors may be helpful. Both the individual items and the factors were generated initially a priori. Subsequently, individual items and factors were refined through a process of review— first by a panel of professional experts in survey design and then by a panel of human resource managers participating in a pilot study of the instrument.

The current set of factors was determined by factor analysis of the data from over 12,000 respondents representing a broad cross section of organizations. More than 50 private sector and public sector organizations are now represented in the norm pool, which includes electronics manufacturing, retail, banking, professional, research and development, agricultural, hospitality industry, consumer goods manufacturing, resort operation, and governmental organizations. The sizes of the groups studied range from about 50 to over 4000 employees.

The reliability of the overall instrument and of the individual factors was determined using Cronbach's Alpha, a statistic widely accepted as a general-purpose measure of reliability. The alpha coefficients calculated for the total instrument and for the individual factors are shown in Exhibit 6-2. The reliabilities ranging from 0.757 to 0.929 were judged to be more than satisfactory to justify further use of the instrument.

The validity of the instrument was determined on the basis of content validity. Since no equivalent instrument with previously validated factors is known to exist, it was not possible to determine predictive validity through correlation with a criterion measure.

Exhibit 6-2 *Coefficient Alpha Reliabilities*

Scale	Alpha Coefficient
Total Instrument	0.978
Factors:	
Reward system	0.774
Communication	0.894
Organization effectiveness	0.901
Concern for people	0.828
Organizational objectives	0.874
Cooperation	0.852
Intrinsic satisfaction	0.888
Structure	0.757
Relationships	0.765
Climate	0.929
Participation	0.852
Work group	0.766
Intergroup competence	0.799
Quality of management	0.866

Moreover, content validation seems the more reasonable approach for an instrument consisting of items directly reporting an individual's perceptions and attitudes. There are two expert judgments involved in content validity: (a) the extent to which each item in a trait or factor scale pertains to the factor as it is defined, and (b) the extent to which the entire set of items represents all aspects of the factor. Each of the factors of the *HRI* was judged to be "highly valid" by a panel of survey design experts and personnel managers.

WHAT ARE THE USES OF THE *HRI*?

The *Human Resources Index* has been used in firms representing a wide range of industries and sizes. Norms have been developed that are proving remarkably stable. Although considerable variation is seen in comparing one organization with another, whenever large numbers of responses are aggregated, the results are surprisingly consistent. The present norms for the 15 factors are represented graphically in Exhibit 6-3. A sample printout of data from the *HRI* is shown in Exhibit 6-4.

Exhibit 6-3 Human Resources Index *Norms*

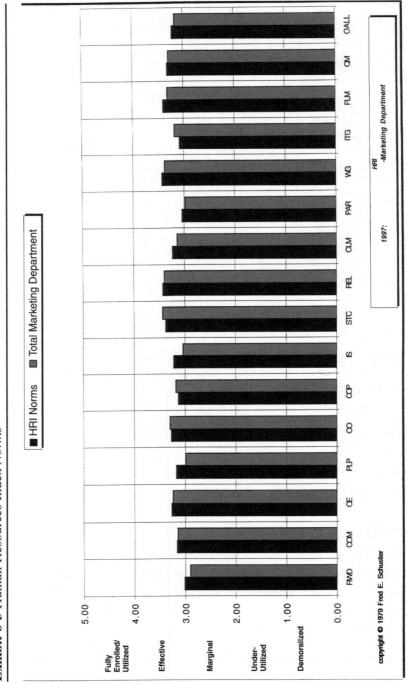

Exhibit 6-4 *Excerpts from* Human Resources Index *Computer Printout*

SORT 1: Gender	0	0
SORT 2: Full Time/Part Time	0	0
SORT 3: Years of Service	0	0
SORT 4: Job Grade	0	0
SORT 5: Division	0	0

1997:   -MARKETING DEPARTMENT

	N=9041 HRI NORMS	1997 Total Marketing N=242	
F1: Reward System	3.01	2.90	S
F2: Communication	3.16	3.15	
F3: Organization Effectiveness	3.26	3.24	S
F4: Concern for People	3.17	2.99	
F5: Organization Objectives	3.27	3.30	S
F6: Cooperation	3.13	3.18	S
F7: Intrinsic Satisfaction	3.22	3.04	S
F8: Structure	3.38	3.44	
F9: Relationships	3.43	3.40	
F10: Climate	3.23	3.14	S
F11: Participation	3.04	2.98	S
F12: Work Group	3.43	3.38	
F13: Inter-group Competence	3.08	3.18	S
F14: First Level Supervision	3.40	3.31	
F15: Quality of Management	3.31	3.29	
Overall	3.21	3.16	S

Perhaps the most important conclusion that can be reached from the work that has been done on the *Human Resources Index* is that such a survey can be quite practical as a means for evaluating how effectively an organization is managing its human resources. Moreover, the survey data have proved highly useful in diagnosing specific problems requiring concentrated attention and in initiating organization development by opening up two-way communication about matters of practical significance to the organization.

NOTES

1.   Hajime Karatsu, "The 'Japan Bashers' Are Wrong," *Pacific Basin Quarterly*, Pacific Basin Center Foundation, 1984, no. 11.
2.   Yoshi Tsurumi, "The Japanese Conspiracy: A New Hoax on the American Public," *Pacific Basin Quarterly*, 1984, no. 11.

7 ACTING ON KEY OPPORTUNITIES FOR IMPROVEMENT: STEP 2 OF STRATEGY A

Once the climate survey data have been studied carefully, it should be easy for the chief executive and his or her immediate subordinates to identify at least a few key opportunities for immediate improvement. These are typically conditions or policies about which there is widely recognized dissatisfaction or confusion (some of these could perhaps have been identified by the top management group before the survey was conducted). The top candidates, or "winners," to highlight for immediate action have a high payout/investment ratio and a short payout period. Almost all organizations have a few such opportunities waiting to be exploited, and now that they have been broadly recognized as a result of the survey, the time is ripe for taking action. Each organization will develop its own list, but the key factor is that action must begin immediately on at least a few hot issues.

In one organization with which I have worked, a climate survey revealed that the single largest complaint people had (voiced by 70 percent of all employees) concerned conditions in the parking lot. It was unpaved and rocky, alternately dusty and muddy, and parking spaces were not marked off. Everybody was unhappy, especially the women, who complained bitterly about ruining their shoes. The top management responded by announcing immediately that the lot would be paved and marked; two days later the paving machinery was in action. The immediate surge of good will and enhanced credibility for the company's carefully planned program to move toward participative management paid back many times the relatively modest cost. Moreover, the chief executive indicated privately that the company had long planned to pave the lot; they just had not gotten around to it because nobody thought it was a high-priority item. In this example, the speed of response was probably far more significant than the amount of money spent by the company in determining the reaction of the workforce. The move is still paying dividends years later, because whenever groups of employees discuss the latest annual climate survey, somebody always mentions the parking lot episode with obvious pride and satisfaction.

Another memorable incident occurred in a savings and loan association when the vast majority of customer contact personnel requested that the association adopt uniforms for both men and women employees who regularly met clients. Essentially, they all felt that uniforms would be both more convenient and less expensive to buy and maintain; moreover, the women felt that the uniforms would eliminate the "competition" over dressing, which many felt had gotten out of hand. Ironically, the president of the association had been wondering for months how to broach the subject of instituting uniforms, which he felt would greatly upgrade the image of the association, but which he feared the staff would stoutly resist. When he announced the new uniform policy and indicated that the association would pay half the cost of uniforms, the employees were delighted. When he announced a few days later that a "name" designer had been contracted to make some prototype designs, and that a fashion show using association *employees* as models would be held so that everyone could *vote* on the uniforms to be selected, pandemonium broke loose. Again, a relatively modest expenditure in the right circumstances and *in response to the initiative of the rank-and-file employees* had paid huge dividends in improved morale, commitment, motivation, and organizational climate. The organization was positioned and poised for rapid improvement on many operational fronts, including productivity.

Opportunities that present themselves in each organization will be unique; however, some especially likely candidates that will arise in many organizations are:

- Improving communication, especially regarding organization goals and objectives
- Increasing participation of all ranks of employees in important management decisions

- Rationalizing the *distribution* of rewards by really linking pay and other rewards directly to performance
- Implementing a flexible compensation program that allows each employee to custom-tailor the mix of compensation and fringe benefits to match personal preferences and needs
- Adopting a productivity bonus plan that allows employees to share tangibly and directly in the improved financial results from *their* successful efforts to increase productivity

Each of these high-potential opportunities for improvement will be discussed at some length in this chapter.

THE CRUCIAL ROLE OF COMMUNICATION

In the typical organization, the primary opportunity for improving performance may turn out to be improving communication, especially increasing the amount of information available to employees concerning organization plans, goals, and objectives. Since "talk is cheap," it often costs very little to launch a rather complete and sophisticated employee communication program including formal and informal, downward, upward, and lateral communication.

Seemingly, keeping people informed about what is going on in the organization should be considered a basic fundamental of good management. Yet ironically, in organization after organization all over America, the most common complaints that surface in climate surveys are:

"I don't know what my boss expects of me."
"I don't know enough about company goals and objectives to rationally plan and run my own job."
"I wish I could hear about company changes and plans at work before I read about them in the newspapers."

Clearly, in many organizations, communication is the weakest link in the management system. This is also perhaps the aspect of management in which the Japanese most excel. If we were to pick one characteristic that most differentiates the Japanese management style from that of the typical American organization, it would undoubtedly be this matter of the attention paid to communication.

American executives pride themselves on being "dynamic" decision makers. Of course, their decisions often fail to be carried out or are sabotaged. Japanese executives, on the other hand, take maddeningly long to make decisions because they insist that everyone be informed and involved; they refuse to commit to a decision until it has been understood and preaccepted by all those who will carry the decision out. As a result, once they make a decision it frequently is executed flawlessly and almost immediately.

One senior manager, when asked to name the internal issue that would have the greatest impact on management over the next five years, replied: "The adequacy and totality (up and down) of communication to ensure that everyone will know what we want to do as a company and what each must provide to ensure that we get there."

The cost of a sophisticated and complete communication program can be relatively modest, but the value of the results produced can be substantial. This is a reality discovered long ago by the Japanese, but only recently has it become widely recognized in American industry. In fact, emphasis on communication is the thread of consistency that ties together the seemingly disparate Japanese practices of decision making through consensus, de-emphasis of status difference and status symbols, quality circles, open office landscaping, and extensive off-the-job socialization of all levels of employees. The Japanese simply practice the belief that effective organized activity stems from full sharing of all information about the organization (both upward and downward) through constantly open channels of communication.

Although such attention to communication is admittedly time consuming, the Japanese believe this is a necessary investment in order to produce commitment, motivation, and maximum contribution from each individual. Some major American corporations, among them Motorola and General Motors, have recently begun to adopt this point of view as part of their extensive efforts to become more competitive with their Japanese counterparts.

Some important elements in a well-rounded formal communication system are:

Orientation programs
Employee handbooks
Bulletins
Official reports
Newsletters
Bulletin boards and posters
Job postings
Policy and procedure manuals

Open forums
Suggestion systems
Attitude surveys
Regular staff and committee meetings
Grievance procedures

Management consultant Scott Myers tells a story that shows how simple—yet complex—the communication function is. He was called in by a client to suggest ways management might communicate better with its workforce. The company, always run along traditional lines, was trying to update itself and its communication practices. Before retaining Myers, management had decided to stress the traditional media methods—more articles in the company paper on corporate objectives and employee benefits, improvement of bulletin board displays, and a new monthly letter from the president.

However, in his initial talk with the president, Myers learned that the company was about to spend almost $300,000 to install what it saw as the most effective and up-to-date way to transmit messages to employees: closed-circuit television monitors scattered throughout the premises. Myers, dismayed by this news, asked for a short delay of the order until he could size up the situation and make some recommendations. The president reluctantly agreed.

In the course of examining the organization's communication efforts, Myers discovered an interesting practice. For some years, employees had a common coffee break during which all coffee machines were programmed to dispense the beverage free. At the same time, a cart carrying free pastries for everyone was wheeled into each area.

Watching the proceedings one morning, Myers recognized an opportunity. At his next meeting with the president, Myers suggested that he join his people out in the corridor at a coffee bar. The president smiled patiently and said he couldn't do that. When asked why not, he replied that "it simply isn't done." Top officers all had their coffee in their own offices, dispensed from a mahogany cart. They never mingled with other employees during breaks. It would have been bad form and might even constitute an intrusion.

Myers persisted, however, and reluctantly the president agreed to try the radical idea. His first attempt was an abysmal failure. He didn't even know how to work the coffee machine. A bystander, seeing him fumble with coins, walked over and told him the coffee was free. Red-faced, he took the cup in hand and looked for someone to begin a conversation with. No one approached him; employees were clustered in little groups quietly discussing their various concerns and glancing curiously at him. He drank his coffee and walked back into his office.

To Myers he pronounced the experiment a flop—employees wouldn't talk to him. Myers told him that the problem was twofold. The president made his appearance too formal; instead of wearing his suit jacket, he should have gone out in his shirtsleeves. Moreover, the workers weren't used to seeing him in their area. To make this a fair test, Myers urged, he must go back tomorrow. At first the president was emphatic in his refusal to subject himself again to such humiliation. Eventually he agreed to try it one more time, but without his suit jacket.

This time the president got his coffee without incident and mustered the courage to break into the perimeter of a small gathering. After some conversation about the weather, he asked how things were going and heard some pleasantries from the group indicating that everything was fine.

The following morning, after doing some homework on a current concern of the workforce (the opening of a plant in Europe), he raised the subject with a coffee-break group and explained the logic behind the decision. He was surprised to find himself in the middle of an animated discussion about the plant.

The next day and the next the president went out to the corridor for his morning coffee. In time he found himself holding forth on all kinds of company issues with employees, who now felt comfortable enough to air their concerns. The kaffeeklatsches were working so well that he asked his senior staff to begin mingling with their people at coffee time. He also canceled the TV equipment in favor of the simpler and more effective technique of firsthand, face-to-face communication.[1]

In one experimental program, General Motors Corporation has used the communication process as a basis for solving some serious problems of worker resentment and alienation. GM management concludes that it is difficult to single out accurately the effects of the communication program from a multitude of factors affecting the organization. But, based on some formal measures of organizational effectiveness and informal feedback from the workers as well as from supervisory personnel, it appears that the communication program has played a major role in improving the organizational climate and worker relations.

At Advanced Micro Devices, every employee has been trained to use computer terminals spread throughout the plant to obtain updated information about product yields, production rates, and any other information about the operation.

Hewlett-Packard uses a variety of techniques to encourage communication with its employees. An important element of this approach is an open-door policy. In many Hewlett-Packard locations, there literally are no doors to individual offices, and top executives, including the president, have offices in large open areas that are divided only by free-standing low partitions. "Management by walking around" was developed as a concept primarily to promote open and frequent communication. Moreover, in most plants, administrative and manufacturing operations are located in the same area to facilitate frequent contact. Common coffee breaks, with the coffee and doughnuts supplied by the company, also support communication. Managers and nonmanagers are thus encouraged to know each other, and informal discussion of projects and problems is facilitated. For the same reason, the company sponsors afternoon "beer busts" and picnics for the whole plant. "Management by walking around" encourages managers to spend a part of each day wandering through the organization without any specific purpose other than to see what is going on and to build new channels of communication with other employees.

At Delta Air Lines, communication is thought to be a key to maintaining a successful operation, and the company has many programs for keeping in touch with employees. Small groups of employees meet periodically with top management of their departments for a free and open exchange of opinions. When employees complained about worn-out waiting room furniture at one sales office, the furniture was changed within weeks.

THE POWER OF PARTICIPATION

One nearly sure-fire method to improve productivity is to increase participation of rank-and-file employees in important management decisions. Lack of sufficient opportunity to participate is the single complaint voiced most frequently by workers in organizations across America.

Worker participation in planning bids for new contracts at Harman-International, and work teams at Donnelly Mirrors (Donnelly Corporation) determining their own pay, are both examples of rank-and-file participation in action. General Electric has implemented a grievance review process in a *nonunion* facility in which the controlling majority of the grievance panel (with authority to bind the company) consists of rank-and-file production employees.

John Naisbitt points out in *Megatrends* that there is a fundamental mismatch between the traditional American love of personal liberty and the top-down, authoritarian management style characteristic of American executives. Naisbitt comments:

Traditional American management has adopted an insulting top-down approach to a worker's knowledge in his or her job. Managers in the United States have consistently denied workers the opportunity to make substantive decisions about how their jobs should be done. Only now are we beginning to see that this elitist strategy has cost America top honors in world productivity growth. . . . For at least the past three decades American management consultants and behavioral scientists have been trying to push the idea [of employee participation] here, to no avail. American managers thought the idea mushy and unmeasurable and felt certain it would have no impact on the almighty bottom line. Meanwhile U.S. productivity gains slid, high quality imports gained a greater and greater U. S. market share, and American companies finally had to ask themselves: "What are we doing wrong?" Only at that point was the door opened for increased worker participation.

Naisbitt concludes that:

As we grew to recognize our new place in a world economy, we came face to face with our Japanese competitors, only to learn that the management structure that made them the world's leading industrial power was anything but pyramidal in nature; instead, Japanese workers, clustered into small decentralized work groups, made work decisions themselves, and the people on top received their word as something resembling gospel. As we introduced more technology into society, the cold impersonal nature of the bureaucratic hierarchy annoyed people more and more. What we really wanted was more personal interaction, more high-touch ballast in response to the further intrusion of technology into an already impersonal hierarchy. Finally, younger, more educated and rights-conscious workers began filling up the workplace. Raised to take seriously the ideology of democracy . . . the whole notion of hierarchy and pyramids was to them foreign, unnatural.[2]

In an experiment in one Ford Motor Company assembly plant, every worker on the assembly line was given access to a button that could be pushed to shut down the line. The people actually shut down the facility 30 times during the first day and about 10 times a day thereafter. After the first day, however, the average shutdown lasted only about 10 seconds—just enough time to make a needed correction or small adjustment. The important finding, however, was that *productivity in the plant did not change.* Apparently there were enough productivity improvements to counterbalance the time lost during the shutdowns. More important, the number of defects per car produced dropped during the first months of the experiment from 17.1 per car to 0.8 per car. Cars needing rework fell by 97 percent, and the number of grievances dramatically decreased. The company also reported that there was a dramatic improvement in attitudes. One assembly worker commented, "It's like someone opened the window and we can breathe."

Texas Instruments has also reported positive results from giving employees autonomy. Work teams were allowed to set their own targets for production, and executives report that the typical result has been for workers to set goals that require them to stretch but that are reasonable and attainable.

Procter & Gamble estimates that it gets a 30 to 40 percent gain in productivity when operations are managed by self-directed teams, and this produces a sustainable competitive cost advantage. As a matter of fact, when this relationship was first discovered in early experiments in the 1960s, it was declared a trade secret because it produced such a major competitive advantage. These early experiments, incidentally, were directed by Douglas McGregor, who was brought into Procter & Gamble as a consultant.

Other organizations that have reported massive gains in productivity and morale from utilizing self-managing teams are General Mills, Chaparral Steel, Tektronix, Shenandoah Life Insurance, Levi Strauss, Eaton, Monsanto, AT&T, Federal Express, and General Electric.

When Monsanto Chemical Company implemented self-managed teams at one chemical and nylon plant, teams of workers were responsible for hiring, purchasing, job assignment, and production. As a result, management was reduced from seven levels to four, and the plant experienced significant increases in profitability.

At Federal Express, service problems decreased 13 percent after the company's clerical workers were organized in teams and given additional training and authority. At AT&T costs were reduced by more than 30 percent at one plant through the use of teams.

When it was time to purchase new forklift trucks at a Levi Strauss plant, the drivers themselves were involved in the decision. They determined the specifications, negotiated with suppliers, and made the final purchase decision. As a result, the company saved a significant amount of money and also obtained more suitable equipment.

At Eaton, teams of workers were involved in building two new automated machines instead of going to an outside vendor. The company calculates that the machines cost less than a third of what they would have paid to an outside vendor, and the output of the department doubled in the first year.

Rene McPherson, former CEO of Dana Corporation, says: "People should be involved in setting their own goals and judging their own performance. The people who know best how the job should be done are the ones doing it." He has also written:

Until we believe that the expert in any particular job is most often the person performing it, we shall forever limit the potential of that person in terms of both his contribution to the organization and his personal development. . . . Within a 25-square-foot area, nobody knows more about how to operate a machine, maximize its output, improve its quality, optimize the material flow, and keep it operating efficiently than do the machine operators, material handlers, and maintenance people responsible for it.

MOTIVATING IMPROVED WORK PERFORMANCE BY TYING PAY DIRECTLY TO PERFORMANCE

Another key opportunity for improving motivation and performance that will surface in many organizations is forging a closer link between individual (or group) contribution and compensation.

Richard Kopelman, Leon Reinharth, and Adam Beer have reported from their research at a large financial institution: "Those branches with a strong tie between performance and rewards achieved significantly higher levels of performance than did those branches with a weak tie between performance and rewards." It is abundantly clear from numerous studies that pay is by far the most powerful motivator of improved work performance.

For this reason, no single function of management offers more opportunity for improving productivity than the administration of the reward system. In the past, many organizations have not put great emphasis on getting the maximum motivational impact from the rewards offered. The 1990s should be a truly revolutionary time in America with regard to administration of compensation.

In most organizations, compensation increases are determined by the following factors, although the weight given to each factor may vary widely from organization to organization or from time to time:

- Changes in the cost of living as measured by the Bureau of Labor Statistics of the Department of Labor
- Adjustments occasioned by changes in the wage structure as a result of changing jobs in the organization or changing relationships between jobs
- Adjustments upward of the whole structure as a result of compensation and benefit surveys
- Seniority or step adjustments
- Adjustments related to the appraisal of individual or group performance ("merit")
- Profitability of the company—that is, ability to pay

Although it is currently a practice in only a few organizations, it is important for motivational purposes to make explicit the determinants of pay for each individual or group, particularly the portion of pay that is based on performance. This is often deliberately avoided or glossed over in order to "avoid hurting people's feelings," but this omission is a serious mistake.

If an organization is currently using a merit pay system, it might be useful to make a quality check by asking employees what they think via an attitude survey. This last step is the ultimate criterion— for there is just no sense in awarding increases and not knowing *objectively* how they are received.

A considerable body of research shows that for rewards to be an effective motivator it is important that employees perceive a direct relationship between performance and the attainment of desired rewards. This means that the mere establishment of an adequate reward system does not provide the basis for employee motivation. It is equally important that the system be communicated in such a way that each employee perceives that the attainment of desired rewards flows directly from successful performance.

One of the important lines of research leading to this conclusion is operant conditioning theory, developed by B. F. Skinner. Operant conditioning theory observes that, among both animals and human beings, behavior that is rewarded tends to be repeated and behavior that is not rewarded tends not to be repeated. Separate, though complementary, lines of research leading to the same conclusion are the expectancy theory of Vroom and the path-goal theory of Porter and Lawler.

Thus, most widely accepted theories of motivation and the empirical evidence from research in organizations all seem to lead to the conclusion that effectiveness in motivating human performance requires:

- A clear statement of the direct relationship between behaviors and anticipated rewards
- An accurate performance appraisal system and an effective merit increase plan that assure that performance will be accurately measured, and that rewards received will be directly commensurate with objectively measured performance
- Effective communication that makes the existence of the appraisal system and merit plan widely known and understood throughout the organization

Although some studies (notably those of Herzberg) have seemed to indicate that money has little value as a motivator and that it can act primarily as a source of dissatisfaction, the vast majority of other studies have concluded that money can act as a very powerful motivator. The explanation of these apparently inconsistent findings lies in the notion that the motivational value of money depends upon the individual's perception of the total situation. Where pay is closely tied to achievement and is seen by others in the organization as a form of recognition, it operates as a very potent motivator indeed. On the other hand, in organizations where there is little perceived relationship between performance and compensation, where pay is not used as an incentive, money may very well have no effect whatsoever as a motivator and may serve only as a source of dissatisfaction.

Furthermore, research by J. Stacy Adams has shown that for a reward system to be effective in motivating behavior, it is necessary that employees perceive the system to operate equitably. For this perception to exist, "inputs" (which include such factors as age, education, skill, seniority, status, and effort expended) should relate to "outcomes" (rewards) in the same way that the individual perceives them to relate for others. Adams' research has shown that people do, in fact, adjust their input to the perceived equity of their rewards. This finding explains clearly the cause of halfhearted, slipshod performance that is an all too familiar phenomenon in many organizations.

At Whole Foods Markets, a grocery chain selling natural foods and nutritional supplements, the company's emphasis on teams is reflected in team-based rewards. Company policy sets the CEO's salary at eight times what the average employee earns, and rewards are based on team performance rather than individual performance. Similarly, in order to build a team-oriented culture, Southwest Airlines places emphasis in its compensation system on profit-sharing and stock ownership rather than individual merit pay.

MAXIMIZING THE ROI IN COMPENSATION THROUGH FLEXIBILITY

A flexible compensation program allows each employee to custom-tailor the mix of compensation and fringe benefit options to match personal preferences and obligations. This approach enables the company to get 100 percent of motivational value for every dollar spent on compensation and benefits.

Traditional approaches to compensation and benefits have been based on the assumption that most employees in an organization are essentially alike in their needs, their motivations, and their responses to different types of rewards. A contingency approach assumes, on the other hand, that employees are quite different—that some respond primarily to extrinsic rewards (pay), that others respond primarily to intrinsic rewards (achievement), and that still others respond best to a combination of extrinsic and intrinsic rewards. A number of research studies have indicated that both individuals and groups differ in terms of the perceived importance of pay and the effectiveness of money as a motivator. Furthermore, a contingency approach recognizes that, although all employees probably seek "equity," there may be many conflicting definitions of "equity," so that what will appear equitable to one employee may not necessarily appear equitable to another.

An excellent means to facilitate a contingency-based reward system is "flexible compensation" or, as it is sometimes called, "cafeteria compensation." Flexible compensation gives each individual a number of options as to the form and timing of his or her total compensation package, instead of informing the individual of the company's unilateral decision regarding the portion of total compensation that will be given in the form of cash, a retirement plan, life insurance, vacation time, and so forth. The employee is told how many compensation cost units have been granted and perhaps also the required minimums in such areas as cash compensation, retirement, and health insurance. Employees are then allowed to use remaining compensation units to "shop" from among the options offered, much as they would select a meal in a cafeteria.

The cafeteria approach appears to have a number of practical advantages. First of all, the organization can supply an array of equal-cost alternative rewards and allow each individual (within limits) to select his or her own preferred mix. This, of course, will maximize each individual's opportunity to choose rewards that meet his or her own needs and preferences. Moreover, although the cost to the company remains the same regardless of the combinations chosen, the psychological value of the reward for each individual should be higher since he or she is getting 100 percent of the rewards that are of greatest value and none of the rewards that would represent a cost to the company but be of little or no value to the individual. Psychologically, this is like giving the employee a raise at no cost to the company. Another value of this approach is that it allows employees to participate in a vital decision that relates to their jobs. This opportunity to play a decision-making role rather than a passive role in a job-related area of vital concern is itself a satisfier of higher-level needs and thus should have its own motivational impact.

The cafeteria approach also makes obvious to employees the economic value of each fringe benefit they choose. In many organizations this is no small matter. A number of research studies have shown that employees often grossly underestimate the cost, and therefore the economic value, of the fringe benefits supplied by their employers. Since they underestimate the cost of the company-supplied fringe benefits, they underestimate the total compensation they receive. The flexible compensation approach makes this unfortunate result virtually impossible.

None of the practical constraints and problems that need to be addressed in implementing flexible compensation are insurmountable. However, the matter of tax treatment for optional benefits will require careful attention. In order to maximize the tax advantages of benefits it will be necessary to plan carefully and perhaps to work directly with the IRS in arranging options that will meet the IRS tests for favorable tax treatment.

Another area of difficulty is adverse selection of certain insurance coverages. It will be necessary to provide either minimum levels of coverage for all employees or medical qualifications for higher coverage to avoid the problem under voluntary participation that only employees anticipating heavy medical expenses would elect the highest levels of medical insurance coverage. One solution for adverse selection of life insurance is to charge differential rates based on attained age rather than a standard rate for all employees.

Thus, the practical problems that must be worked out to make flexible compensation operational have generally proven to be solvable. Because of the many advantages described here, widespread adoption of flexible compensation has been one of the major trends of the last ten years; it will probably continue to be a strong trend for some time to come.

Another real advantage of flexible compensation is that it involves the individual in important decisions concerning his or her pay. Flexible compensation represents an expression by management of confidence and trust in the individual employee. At the same time, it allows an employee to custom-tailor pay and benefits in order to maximize the value of the reward package to the individual employee. Flexible compensation, thus, has both economic and psychological value to the employee as a step away from paternalism and toward participation/independence. Research by Ed Lawler (1992) points out that one of the advantages of such an approach is that "employees are more likely to trust a pay system of their own design because they have more control over it."

THE DIRECT APPROACH: PAYING PEOPLE TO IMPROVE PRODUCTIVITY

Most organizations should seriously consider a plan to reward employees directly for increases in productivity. Productivity bonus plans such as the Scanlon Plan provide incentive compensation based on organization performance. Their primary emphasis is to stimulate management/union or management/worker cooperation. They do this by setting up a series of joint committees consisting of representatives selected by management and by workers in each department. These committees review suggestions for the improvement of productivity. Suggestions adopted by the committees are implemented in the organization. Of course, not all suggestions can be adopted; but it is important to report back a logical reason when any suggestion is deemed impractical.

When increases in productive efficiency are realized—that is, when unit labor costs decrease—employees and stockholders share the dollar value of the savings according to a predetermined formula.

The major objectives of the Scanlon Plan are to stimulate worker ideas for improving efficiency, to gain the commitment of all employees to the objective of efficiency, to improve employee/management relations, and to provide an equitable basis for sharing the financial rewards of improved efficiency. The Donnelly Mirrors Corporation, for example, has a comprehensive reward system that includes both a productivity bonus (Scanlon Plan) and profit sharing, in addition to competitive base salaries and fringe benefits.

Performance bonuses are similar to productivity bonuses except that they are paid for total performance, including performance that goes beyond mere productivity. Any measurable item of performance can be subject to such bonuses. Thus, performance bonuses can be applied to executive, professional, technical, clerical, white-collar, and blue-collar workers.

Profit-sharing plans typically provide that a stated percentage of profits will be shared by all employees of the organization or by certain groups in the organization. Profits can be shared on a level percentage basis beginning with the first dollar of profit, but a more popular arrangement is to share an increasing percentage of the profits beyond a certain minimum. The timing of payment may be current, deferred, or mixed. Notice that while productivity plans pay a bonus for increases in productivity without regard to changes in profits, profit-sharing plans pay for increases in profits that may reflect many things other than improvements in productivity. For this reason, many organizations may find it worthwhile to have *both* productivity-sharing and profit-sharing plans.

Dana Corporation has used productivity bonus plans for years, and approximately two-thirds of its plans are variations of the Scanlon Plan. Before a plan is adopted, at least three-quarters of a plant's workers have to vote for it. If the plan results in productivity improvements, the workers receive a bonus equal to 75 percent of the savings, and the company gets the other 25 percent.

Dana Corporation also has a cash profit-sharing plan. Under this plan, the company distributes 12 percent of pretax profit to employees, with the same percentage of base salary paid to each employee as a bonus.

Levi Strauss Corporation has also utilized a gain-sharing program with great success. If employees make a suggestion that saves the factory money they receive half the profits generated by the idea. Needless to say, employees are both satisfied and motivated by this arrangement; but the company figures it is the biggest winner.

Lincoln Electric is famous for its piecework and incentive bonus plan. The factory workforce is paid on a piecework basis, and workers are paid only for production that passes quality inspection. Workers correct quality problems on their own time. Moreover, each product carries the name of the individual who made it; if it comes back later with a manufacturing defect, the worker is not paid for repairing it. Needless to say, both quality and productivity are exceptionally high. Bonuses, which are often 100 percent of regular pay, are based on the company's profitability—thus encouraging employees to identify with the whole firm.

Although the experience of firms adopting the Scanlon Plan and other productivity bonus plans has on the whole been extremely positive (for example, the General Accounting Office found the *average* result to be a 17 percent reduction in labor cost, which would be quite significant in most organizations), these plans have not been widely adopted.

This circumstance is both unfortunate and puzzling. The fact is that neither management nor labor in America has eagerly pursued productivity-sharing plans even though both might benefit substantially. (There is some recent evidence in the automobile and airline industries that this attitude may be changing.) Much of the hesitancy within management ranks seems to stem from two primary objections:

1. Resistance to the sharing of influence and power through joint productivity-improvement committees, a resistance based on the untested (and frequently unjustified) assumption that as employees gain influence, executives will somehow lose control and authority
2. Resistance on the part of the board of directors to sharing the dollar value of productivity improvements with employees on the philosophical grounds that any financial benefits from improving performance should belong entirely to the stockholders

The latter point reflects a remarkably shortsighted view because it is equivalent to insisting on one's legal right to 100 percent of nothing in preference to gaining 50 percent of something. Nevertheless, the future growth of productivity-sharing plans seems inevitable as market forces coerce both management and labor to achieve productivity improvement and to limit wage increases to those justified by productivity growth.

This chapter has highlighted five major opportunities (frequently suggested by employees in organizational climate surveys) for implementing increased attention to employees. The key message, however, is the critical importance of taking some action as a direct response to the opportunities for improvement identified in a survey. This is an extremely vital step in Strategy A.

NOTES

1. Adapted from Roger D'Aprix, "The Oldest (and best) Way to Communicate with Employees," *Harvard Business Review*, September–October, 1982.
2. John Naisbitt, *Megatrends: Ten New Directions Transforming Our Lives* (New York: Warner Books, 1982).

8 PAYING EXECUTIVES AND MANAGERS FOR EFFECTIVE MANAGEMENT OF PEOPLE: STEP 3 OF STRATEGY A

All individuals in organizations, including executives and managers, concentrate their attention and their performance on those aspects of the job that are measured and rewarded. Thus, if we wish to transform the organization into one in which executives and managers really pay attention to employee needs (as opposed to the traditional lip service to the importance of employees), it is vital that we change executive evaluation and reward practices so that we begin to measure and pay for effective management of people as well as rewarding for short-term profit. If we really want executives to take the long-term perspective of building the human organization, we have to measure this performance and include it in pay determination. We have to learn to invest for the long term in people as well as equipment. We must move toward measuring performance by long-term results instead of year to year, or even quarter to quarter, and we need to commit our organizations to sacrifice short-term profits for long-term control of markets.

In discussing the lack of relationship between the job performance of top executives and their compensation, a *Fortune* magazine study pointed out that "to an extraordinary extent those who flop still get paid handsomely. In this regard they have something in common with union members who are able to extract higher than market wages from their employers . . . if directors behaved responsibly, they would handle the stockholders' money as if it were their own, avoiding compensation excess" (C.J. Loomis, "The Madness of

Executive Compensation," *Fortune*, July 12, 1982, pp. 42–52). Although this *Fortune* study is now a few years old, top executive pay remains a highly controversial issue, and there have so far been no more recent published results to contradict or modify the conclusions reached.

How should we measure executive performance? One of the reasons it is no longer adequate to measure it solely on the basis of profitability is that it is all too easy to liquidate the human organization, to push people to high levels of performance *in the short run* through coercion, threats, and bullying and thereby generate an increase in profits for one year, possibly even two. The problem with this strategy from the organization's standpoint, however, is that this improvement is apparent, not real; it represents a liquidation of the human assets of the organization rather than an increase in true profitability. Executives who manage in this way are generating a spurious, short-term profit just as if they were selling inventory for 50 cents on the dollar, or allowing valuable machinery to deteriorate from lack of maintenance. Most managers have seen at least a few of these "fast track" individuals in action—people who build successful careers on the basis of destroying an organization to achieve short-run profitability. They then move along to the next promotion before the disaster becomes apparent, leaving the wreckage behind for someone else to salvage.

Hence, it is necessary that we measure and reward effective management of people both to prevent the liquidation of the human organization and to motivate attention to its long-term development as a strategy for improving performance and profitability. This is, in fact, the strategy characteristic of many Japanese organizations. Unlike their American counterparts, Japanese corporate leaders focus attention on building an effective organization and on maximizing profits over the long term through control and domination of their markets. In the course of pursuing this strategy, they are quite willing to forgo maximizing profits in any one- or two-year span, and they are willing to tolerate minimal profits or even losses for extended periods of time (sometimes as long as five or ten years) in pursuit of their ultimate strategy of penetrating and then dominating a major new market. This is precisely the strategy the Japanese followed in taking over the manufacture of color television sets from American firms, and the strategy they followed to make their major penetration into the automobile industry.

LONG-TERM VERSUS SHORT-TERM FOCUS

Japanese executives and managers are free to emphasize long-term performance because their annual compensation is not determined on the basis of profitability in a one-year period. To the extent that productivity and profitability figure into executive compensation in Japan, they are usually evaluated on the basis of performance over a span of at least five or ten years. On a short-term basis, the main aspect of a Japanese executive's performance that is evaluated and rewarded is his or her ability to manage people effectively—that is, the ability to communicate with employees and the ability to generate high levels of commitment, understanding, motivation, and morale. The Japanese assume that these organizational characteristics are the basic building blocks for long-term performance and profitability, along with, of course, careful attention to strategic planning.

By contrast, in the typical American organization the compensation of executives and managers is closely tied into short-term results. Some top executives have their annual bonuses tied almost entirely to single-year profitability, and these bonuses may represent two-thirds or more of their total compensation. Even middle-level managers may have one-third of their total compensation wrapped up in an annual bonus that is determined almost entirely by profitability. Thus, even those managers and executives who would like to take an enlightened long-term view are virtually prevented from doing so by the reward system, which will punish them for building an organization for long-term performance through attention to employees, while rewarding their colleagues for destroying the human organization in order to achieve short-term performance.

Reginald Jones, former board chairman and CEO of the General Electric Company, says that "too many managers feel under pressure to concentrate on the short term in order to satisfy the financial community and owners of the enterprise, the stockholders. In the United States, if your firm has a bad quarter, it's headlines. Real trouble ensues. The stock price falls out of bed. That's far different from Japan and Germany."

Very few American corporations have truly long-term compensation plans for their executives, and year-end bonuses are almost universally larger than long-term incentives. "What short-term CEO will take a long-run view when it lowers his own income?" asks economist Lester Thurow. "Only a saint, and there aren't very many saints."

John Naisbitt points out in *Megatrends* that "in most corporations, middle-management executives are responsible for identifiable profit centers and are promoted or demoted based on quarterly profits. The product-manager system is notorious for this. The sum of it is that everybody works to get immediate results, not only ignoring the longer-range future, but often at the expense of the future."

The short term and frequently shortsighted positions win out with disturbing regularity because American business is top heavy with the ever-expanding number of business school graduates who are trained advocates of short-term profit. As Jeffrey Pfeffer (1994) points out:

The bad news about achieving some competitive advantage through the workforce is that it inevitably takes time to accomplish. By contrast, a new piece of equipment can be quickly installed; a new product technology can be acquired through a licensing agreement in the time it takes to negotiate the agreement; and acquiring capital only requires the successful conclusion of negotiations. The good news, however, is that once achieved, competitive advantage obtained through employment practices is likely to be substantially more enduring and more difficult to duplicate. Nevertheless, the time required to implement these practices and start seeing results means that a long-term perspective is needed. It also takes a long time horizon to execute many of these approaches. In the short term, laying off people is probably more profitable compared to trying to maintain employment security; cutting training is a quick way to maintain short-term profits; and cross-training and cross-utilization may provide insights and innovation in time, but initially, the organization foregoes the advantages of more narrow specialization and the immediate proficiency achieved thereby.

A prime example of the folly of rewarding executives for taking a short-term perspective while hoping that they will take a long-term perspective is provided by the automobile industry. At a time when the industry desperately needs to concentrate its full attention and energies on improving quality, improving productivity, and reducing costs so as to compete more effectively with the Japanese automakers, the executive reward system is instead still focusing executives' attention on maximizing short-term profit at the expense of long-term competitiveness and survival.

In this regard, the auto industry is following closely on the heels of the American steel industry, which for years paid out handsome executive bonuses based on annual profitability, while the industry slowly destroyed itself through failure to hold down labor cost and to modernize plants. The auto industry, which came under heavy criticism in the early 1980s for paying out huge executive bonuses in the midst of an industry crisis, decided in 1984 to pay out even bigger bonuses, based on record profits. Specifically, the payouts totaled $1.8 million for General Motors Corporation Chairman Roger Smith, almost $1.6 million for retired Ford Motor Company Chairman Philip Caldwell, and nearly $1.2 million for Chrysler Corporation Chairman Lee Iacocca. The bonus plans were tied closely into profits during a single year, and profits in both 1983 and 1984 were quite high due to the "voluntary" limitation on the importation of Japanese cars.

Ironically, the whole idea of the "voluntary restraint" was to give the American auto industry a breathing space in order to recoup and reorganize. The intent was to provide a few years of protection while the industry redesigned products, retooled, and changed management practices so that quality could be improved and costs reduced, and so the industry could emerge more competitive.

Instead, because the incentive plan focused executive attention on one-year profits rather than long-term strength and competitiveness, the automakers inevitably concentrated on raising prices and maximizing profits in the period when they were artificially protected from competition. Long-term goals—reducing costs, improving quality—were largely forgotten. As a result, the consumer paid heavily for the record short-term profits and bonuses in the form of higher prices, while the industry emerged from the experience little stronger than before and complaining that it could no longer compete without its protection.

It would be a mistake, however, to blame this fiasco on the executives involved. Their response was rational in relation to the incentives that were presented to them in the bonus program. The real blame lies with the stockholders and boards of directors who were so shortsighted as to tie the reward system into short-term profits. The outcome would have been different if the executives had been rewarded, instead, for building the human organization for the long term, improving morale and climate, improving productivity, and improving quality. Executives do what they are paid to do. If stockholders want long-term performance, it is essential that reward systems be revised to measure and to pay for the factors that lead to it.

Reginald Jones suggests a solution to this dilemma: "Boards of directors have to understand that they must shelter management from these pressures. In the interest of the corporation itself and in the interest of the nation, the board has got to concern itself with the long-range future of the business and not be that upset by a bad quarter so long as productive and cost-effective spending is going on for the long range."

For example, Levi Strauss has said that many of the workforce management changes that have made it enormously profitable could never have been implemented if the firm had not gone private in a leveraged buyout. The primary benefit of the buyout was that it freed management from concern with quarterly results so that the firm could take the long-range view, and this approach has paid off handsomely.

John Naisbitt points out that "the criticism about short-term management is becoming widely accepted by the business community itself. Of nearly 1000 top executives surveyed by the Chicago management research firm, Heidrick and Struggles, 76 percent said there has been a damaging overemphasis on immediate financial goals."

Another tragedy of the auto fiasco is that executive bonuses further alienated workers at the critical time for the industry to move toward greater cooperation. The bonuses were widely resented by the rank and file, who had taken cuts, and they were blasted by UAW executives for "incredible shortsightedness." If the instigators of the bonus system had been concerned with the climate and motivation of the human organization, quality improvement, and greater productivity, it is likely that they would have designed productivity bonus plans (such as the Scanlon Plan) and would have improved communication and cooperation, rather than arranging for one last hurrah for maximizing short-term profits.

Once an organization does make a commitment to abandon the destructive concentration on short-term results, it is not all that difficult to devise a reward system that will lead to a strategy of attention to the needs of employees in order to build a committed, highly motivated work force and an organization with a long-term perspective.

Perhaps the most effective performance planning and evaluation system that has yet been devised for encouraging managers to pay attention to the total job of managing is one that has gone by several names—work planning and review, performance planning, and management by objectives. The name is, of course, unimportant; what matters is that the performance appraisal and reward process be tied into predetermined performance targets, and that performance be appraised on the basis of *objective measures of accom-*

plishment. It is also critical, for the reasons just described, that these performance targets and measures of accomplishment include objective measurement of how good a job the manager is doing in attending to the needs of employees and in eliciting high levels of motivation and commitment from those employees.

MEASURING EXECUTIVE PERFORMANCE

Peter Drucker has proposed a system for measuring executive and managerial performance based on what he calls an annual "manager's letter." In this letter or statement of performance targets, individuals first set down the performance standards that they believe should be applied to measure their performance and contribution. The statement of goals is discussed between the individuals and their superiors until they reach agreement on a final statement summarizing in objective and measurable terms the performance targets and contributions to which the superior plans to hold his or her subordinates responsible for the coming year. If changing business conditions or changing circumstances in either the external or internal environment require it, this statement is modified and updated during the performance year. At the end of the year, the executive's or manager's performance is evaluated objectively on the basis of how well the targets have been achieved.

Perhaps the greatest advantage to the evaluation of the individual manager is that he or she can know in advance exactly what performance and contribution and exactly what standards of performance are expected. There are no hidden agendas and no surprises at the end of the year. Moreover, this system also enables the individual to control his or her own performance; and self-control leads to stronger motivation. Douglas McGregor was very much interested in the relationship between performance appraisal practices and motivation. He strongly supported Drucker's proposal for a new system of performance measurement and set forth a detailed procedure for a motivational approach to performance measurement.

Building on the logic of both Drucker and McGregor, I recommend the following five-step process for planning and measuring the performance of executives and managers:

1. The individual discusses his or her job description with the superior; together they agree on the content of the job and the relative importance of the major duties. The superior establishes a clear

understanding of the things that the subordinate will be held accountable for, that is, the things the subordinate is paid to do.

2. The individual establishes performance targets for each of his or her responsibilities for the forthcoming period.
3. The individual meets with the superior to discuss the draft of the individual's performance target program. They refine and modify the statement of performance targets until they are able to agree on a final statement. If no other course is possible—and it is hoped that such instances can be kept to a minimum—the superior unilaterally assigns the subordinate's targets. The two also agree on checkpoints to be established for evaluating progress, and they agree on the *objective measures* to be used to evaluate performance and contribution.
4. At the end of the performance period (frequently one year), the superior and subordinate meet to evaluate the accomplishment of the targets previously agreed on.
5. All performance rewards (including salary increases, bonuses, stock options, promotions, and so forth) are tied *directly* and *visibly* into the accomplishment of the performance targets and into *nothing else.*

The forms used for this approach by different companies vary considerably, and some companies prefer to use only a blank sheet of paper. It is important, however, that the forms emphasize an explicit relationship between the evaluation of performance against objectives and the determination of incentive bonuses. Although it is not yet common to have such a direct and explicit tie between the performance evaluation and the determination of bonuses, it is highly important in order to emphasize long-term goals.

SETTING PERFORMANCE OBJECTIVES FOR EFFECTIVE MANAGEMENT OF PEOPLE AS WELL AS FOR PROFIT, EFFICIENCY, AND GROWTH

In addition to targets for traditional performance measures such as profitability, cost control, and quality, there should also be objective measures of how effectively each executive or manager is utilizing his or her human resources, and how effectively he or she is building the morale and commitment of the human organization. As discussed earlier, it is essential that these measures also be included in the performance evaluation if we are to realistically expect managers and executives to put a balanced amount of emphasis on this aspect of performance. The precise measures most meaningful in a particular organization will, of course, depend on the individual circumstances, but it is conceptually not difficult to identify and objectively define the performance areas relevant to building the human organization and its effective utilization.

In the business environment, where financial results are not only measured but given close scrutiny, any failure to measure the implementation and results of a strategy to emphasize the motivation and commitment of the human organization will doom the effort to neglect and failure. Again, all employees including executives tend to emphasize performance of what is measured. The feedback from the measurements is also essential to refine and improve the management strategy.

Hewlett-Packard, for example, does a magnificent job of putting its money where its mouth is. Managers are held accountable not only for their financial results but also for the results of employee attitude surveys. Each measure has equal impact on the managers' pay and career development.

I recommend that, as a minimum, each organization implement a standardized employee survey that is used annually in every division and work unit. The overall index of performance on this survey should be *one* of the job performance areas for which targets are set and to which organizational rewards are directly linked for each manager.

IBM, for example, regularly uses a standardized survey to measure the climate and morale of each organizational unit. The survey includes both those items that are used in common with other organizations in the Mayflower Group (a group of companies that compare survey data) and a number of specific items developed internally for use within IBM. The data that result are then routinely used as one of the objective measures of performance for each executive and manager, who is also evaluated on the basis of such objective measures as turnover, performance improvement of subordinates, and development of subordinates for promotion. While IBM executives and managers are never allowed to lose sight of the financial targets, it is also true that they cannot succeed within the organization just by achieving those financial targets, if it is at the expense of the morale, commitment, and motivation of the human organization. In order to advance within managerial and executive ranks at IBM, it is important to achieve balanced accomplishment in all of the performance areas that are measured.

Each manager should be made aware that performance on the objective index of human resource management will receive equal weight with the other performance targets that have been established. Some other measures of attention to the human organization are turnover (looking not just at numbers, but at the quality of those who voluntarily terminate); performance appraisal trends of subordinates; number of positions within the unit for which there is adequate backup; number of positions filled internally through promotion versus the number that must be filled from outside the unit; grievances or complaints; grievances or complaints in which the initial decision of the manager or executive is overturned; and absence statistics. Others will become apparent as the program is put into effect.

Two companies that have been highly successful in truly tying executive pay to the effective management of people are Hyatt Hotels and Federal Express. Hyatt performs an annual employee attitude survey, and it is considered the one thing that can make or break a hotel manager's career. In addition to using survey results as a major determinant of managers' pay, if a manager receives a series of unsatisfactory survey results he or she will be out the door.

Federal Express also conducts an annual employee attitude survey consisting of twenty-nine questions. Each manager receives a score for each of the questions as well as a total score. The first ten questions comprise what Federal Express calls the "leadership index," and each year goals are set for each manager and for the company on the "leadership index." If the company doesn't make the goal, the top three hundred managers in the company don't get *any* bonus! For top executives, the bonus can represent up to 40 percent of base salary. As you might expect, executives in Federal Express give a very high priority to meeting their employees' needs. Employees feel empowered by this arrangement, and clearly they are.

INCENTIVE PAY PLANS FOR EXECUTIVES AND MANAGERS

Recognition and reward for performance can be in the form of praise (private and public), written commendation, published commendation, increased autonomy, change in job title, performance bonus, salary increase, award of stock options, promotion in grade, increase in responsibilities, and various forms of supplementary compensation and perquisites.

Although the responsibilities of the individual executive and manager remain constant regardless of how performance is evaluated, a considerable body of evidence indicates that, all things being equal, evaluation based on performance objectives is likely to result both in the evaluation itself being more valid and in an increased perception of equity on the part of the individuals evaluated. These would appear to be powerful arguments, indeed, in favor of adopting such an approach to executive and managerial performance evaluation whenever the situation makes it feasible. To the extent that pay is a valued reward, linking it, along with other desirable rewards, to objectively evaluated performance should enhance both motivation and performance.

The effort to find the right approach or the right "system" for executive and managerial performance evaluation must be matched with an effort to create the right climate for that evaluation. Executive evaluation by performance responsibility targets, for example, works best within a climate that emphasizes participation and a high degree of mutual trust and confidence. To be effective as a motivator of performance, the evaluation plan adopted must be viewed by all concerned as consistent with the basic assumptions and style of management prevalent in the organization.

9 BREAKING DOWN THE BARRIERS TO PARTICIPATION, COMMUNICATION, AND CONTRIBUTION: STEP 4 OF STRATEGY A

Many organizations have developed practices and policies that have the effect of erecting artificial barriers to participation, communication, and contribution. Identifying and removing these barriers can be a major source of improvement in organizational performance and productivity. Typically, these barrier-producing practices were developed many years ago in response to some particular need, and may well have served a useful organizational purpose at that time. Unfortunately, they are not often examined to see if they are still relevant; in many instances they have outlived their usefulness. In fact, the harm to the organization that some of these practices may be doing often outweighs any small contribution they may be making.

Among the barriers that an organization might consider eliminating are such previously mentioned divisive symbols as separate dining rooms, reserved parking spaces, elaborate differences in office space and furnishings (that far exceed actual work requirements), and other unnecessary signs of status. In many organizations, careful evaluation of these practices may lead to the conclusion that they are anachronisms, appropriate perhaps to another era, but useless—and even harmful—in the 1990s.

HAVE SOME OF OUR STATUS SYMBOLS
OUTLIVED THEIR USEFULNESS?

Perquisites and status symbols, such as executive dining rooms and washrooms, luxurious private offices, executive cars, and reserved parking spaces, are major barriers to communication within an organization. Using them to reward and differentiate executives may serve as motivators of executive behavior, but they also have the unfortunate side effect of separating, putting down, and demotivating other individuals in the organization. Status symbols are, after all, intended to differentiate people—to set them apart, and to indicate that certain individuals are more valued, more privileged, and more rewarded. In the process of doing this, they quite naturally make others in the organization feel less important, less valued, and less rewarded. They inevitably have the effect of alienating the rest of the workforce. They inhibit communication, block participation, and reduce morale, commitment, and contribution. Thus, the small positive effect they have on the morale and commitment of executives is more than counterbalanced by the negative impact they have on the morale and contribution of the rest of the organization.

Even if the resentment engendered by status symbols did not throw up a psychological barrier to participation and contribution, they directly inhibit communication and participation by symbolizing the unapproachability of managers and executives. Thus, at a time when economic pressures demand that commonality of purpose and cooperation be emphasized, anachronistic status symbols influence the organization in exactly the opposite direction; they stimulate distrust, disunity, and disharmony. Have we not reached a point at which many of these symbols have outlived their usefulness?

For example, do executive dining rooms really contribute more to the organization by providing an opportunity for executives to talk privately together, or do they detract from organizational performance by preventing contact between all levels of the organization, and by creating a sense of alienation and resentment? Do luxurious private offices really contribute more to the organization by facilitating executive performance, or do they detract from the organization by inhibiting executive activity that is now most needed? Do private parking spaces really contribute anything useful to the organization, or do they merely feed the ego of a small number of people at the expense of alienating the majority of the workforce?

ONE LESSON WE *CAN* LEARN FROM THE JAPANESE

As previously mentioned, the single characteristic that best distinguishes the Japanese management style is the constant emphasis on the importance of communication, on the full sharing of information among all members of the organization at all levels, and on securing the voluntary commitment and understanding of all members of the organization before taking action. Japanese executives really believe that they must have the ideas and suggestions of all members of the workforce (even those at the lowest level) in order to make best use of the organization's human assets and maximize organizational performance. To accomplish this objective, they tailor the organization's management practices carefully to encourage participation and the full expression of ideas, and to encourage widespread sharing of information between executives and employees at all levels of the organization. They emphasize creating opportunities for informal communication, and they make a conscious attempt to remove any artificial barriers that tend to get in the way of this vital exchange of information.

The Japanese assume, for example, that differences can best be resolved not through the use of authority or by unilateral executive decision, but by gathering as much information as possible from as many sources as possible. They believe that if all parties are well informed, everyone has an opportunity to adjust to the emerging decision, and all individuals in the organization will be committed to taking needed action once a consensus is reached. Although this approach to organizational decision making is frequently quite lengthy and time consuming, the payoff is that decisions, once made, are quickly and almost automatically implemented with virtually no resistance. By contrast, in the typical American organization decisions may be made "dynamically" in a matter of minutes, but they may never get carried out in practice because of foot dragging and lack of understanding.

A specific example of this Japanese emphasis on decision making through full sharing of information is the quality circle movement, which originated in Japan. Two fundamental assumptions underlie the Japanese use of quality circles:

1. The line worker in direct contact with the job often has detailed information about the work situation and will offer unique and important ideas for planning improvement.

2. Even if the ideas produced by the group are sometimes no better than those that could be produced by the technical staff, the workers are more motivated to carry out the results because they have been personally involved.

There are three Japanese managerial philosophies that incline them toward a humanistic, or Theory Y, approach to management. First, the Japanese tend to view a business organization as a human community serving the needs of many stakeholders—the employees, the executives, and the general public. Profits, while important, are actually viewed as secondary to other objectives, such as meeting employees' needs and providing employment opportunities. This philosophy is supported by the Japanese compensation system, which rewards executives primarily for their effective management of people. It also allows managers and executives to be sensitive to the needs of their employees and to develop a sense of common purpose among all the members of the organization regardless of their rank.

By contrast, American executives tend to see their organizations as primarily economic entities serving the short-run profit objectives of their stockholders. Thus, in America, meeting the needs of employees and the public becomes secondary to the profit motive. As a result, American managers tend to be exploitative.

The second Japanese managerial philosophy involves their view of employees as valuable resources who can make a major difference in organizational performance. Managers and executives in Japan tend to hold Theory Y assumptions about human beings; they assume that their employees are as intelligent and responsible as themselves. As a result, it seems natural to them to rely on workers for solving organizational problems and for contributing voluntarily to high quality and high productivity. By contrast, the most common managerial philosophy in America is still Theory X (though it may be a soft or permissive Theory X). This pessimistic view of their employees' motivation and ability prevents many American managers from utilizing the talents of their workers to the fullest in solving organizational problems.

Finally, Japanese managers tend to believe that the optimal performance of most tasks in large modern organizations requires the cooperation of all organization members. As a result, few decisions of any consequence are imposed unilaterally or made individually. Most happen as a result of group effort. The Japanese really believe that group decisions will tend to be superior decisions technically, and furthermore they will be much more readily implemented. American managers, on the other hand, tend to value individualism much more highly and to see themselves as weak managers if they feel the need for input from others to make decisions. As a result, American executives often pride themselves on their ability to make dynamic decisions, but the price comes when the decision must be implemented. If the organization members have had no input into the planning, they will not be eager to put the new plan into practice.

In order to implement their philosophy of encouraging communication, participation, and contribution, the Japanese have adopted practices that have the effect of removing or playing down status differences that separate people and inhibit communication between individuals at different organizational levels. For example, most Japanese companies do not have separate executive dining rooms. Instead, executives, middle management, and rank-and-file employees all eat in the same cafeteria. This daily mingling with employees has the practical result of opening up two-way communication; top executives hear the ideas and sentiments of their employees and in turn have an opportunity to discuss and explain important organizational decisions. Finally, sharing the cafeteria facilities symbolizes that they are all members of the same team, pursuing a common set of objectives.

For that same reason, many Japanese corporations do not believe in fancy or elaborate offices for even top-level executives. Instead, they sit in large open areas visible to each other and frequently, through glass partitions, even to the rank-and-file employees. Again, this practice is intended to emphasize what all employees in the organization share in common, rather than emphasizing what differentiates them. It tends to encourage Japanese executives and managers to spend a great deal of time walking around the organization. They are constantly standing or sitting at other employees' work stations. They chat with employees regularly and informally about the progress of the organization, its plans and objectives, or the solution of immediate problems. Again, the subtle and subliminal message is that all are members of one team pursuing a unified set of objectives.

Similarly, many Japanese organizations do not provide private parking space for managers and executives. Some even go so far in pursuit of this egalitarian climate as to have all members of the organization, even top-level executives, wear the same standard company uniform. In discussing Honda of America's management practices, the *Wall Street Journal* has reported that:

Employees have also responded well to Honda's efforts to keep them informed of its plans and to solicit their suggestions. . . . As in Japan, Honda here goes out of its way to play down the status distinctions between labor and management and to treat workers as members of a team. Everyone, labor and management, eats in the same company cafeteria, and none of the spaces in the company parking lot are set aside for executives. Employees are called "associates." Instead of ties, executives wear the white Honda uniforms, just as workers do, and as manager Miyano puts it, "The rank of the soldier isn't embroidered on his uniform." Thus, the name tag that purchasing manager Kiochi Nakayama wears identifies him simply as Kiochi. His secretary, Mrs. Wieetelmann, is just "Ann."

There appears to be strong evidence that this approach is paying off for Honda. Although the top executives of Honda of America are Japanese, all of the other employees, middle management as well as the rank and file, are Americans. Nevertheless, at Honda of America, productivity substantially exceeds that of any of the American automobile manufacturers, and quality also exceeds that of the American manufacturers. In fact, it is said that the quality of the Honda automobiles manufactured in the United States is at least as good as the quality of those imported from Japan. When you consider that many of these same workers were previously employed by the big three American automakers, it is clear that the difference in the performance of Honda of America is due to top management and their management practices rather than to any difference in the composition of the workforce. Certainly this example would seem to destroy the myth that the cultural differences of the Japanese blue-collar workers account for their higher productivity and higher quality.

COMPANIES EXEMPLIFYING EGALITARIAN CULTURES

John Naisbitt describes two fast-growing computer firms, Intel and Tandem Computer Co., "where informality is legendary and where executives are stripped of all 'perks' from reserved parking spaces on up." He points out that the most successful new high-tech firms tend to be those that have developed the most high-touch management styles, and he concludes (1982):

But even among the most successful, Tandem is remarkable. The founder of the fast-growing $100 million-a-year company, James Treybig, emphatically states that the human side of the company is the most critical factor in reaching his goal—the $1 billion mark in annual sales. Treybig frees up 100 percent of his personal time to spend on "people projects." Tandem's people-oriented management style includes Friday-afternoon beer parties, employee stock options, flexible work hours (unlike Intel, where everyone is expected to show up promptly at 8:15 A.M.), a company swimming pool that is open from 6 A.M. until 8 P.M., and sabbatical leave every four years—which all employees are *required* to take. Reviews and meetings occur spontaneously with no formal procedures.

Fred K. Foulkes has reported on a research study that examined in detail 26 large corporations that are either predominantly or entirely nonunion. The objective of his study was to determine what characteristics distinguish the nonunion companies from companies with unions, and what characteristics aid these companies in maintaining their nonunion status. Among the companies studied were Black and Decker, Eli Lilly, Gillette, Grumman, Hewlett-Packard, IBM, and Polaroid. It is significant that the first distinguishing characteristic Foulkes discusses is what he calls "a sense of caring." He says:[1]

First and perhaps foremost, many of the founders of the nonunion companies in my sample held fiercely egalitarian views about treatment of employees. Today, many of the customary symbols of corporate rank and status are absent. In many of the companies, everyone from vice president to sweeper has access to the same parking spaces, receives identical medical benefits, and eats in the same cafeteria. Frequently, executive offices are Spartan or even nonexistent. Employees at all levels call each other by their first names.

Moreover, the salaries of some of the top-level executives are modest by *Fortune* "500" standards. Many of these companies eschew such perquisites as company cars and club memberships that symbolize a visible ruling class of management. Top management's commitment to employees is demonstrated not only symbolically but also through certain policies and practices. Hewlett-Packard, for example, is committed to job security, innovative training programs, promotion from within through job posting, cash profit sharing, an attractive stock purchase plan, widely granted stock options, and flexible working hours. In most cases, the founders articulated and put in writing top management's commitment to effective personnel practices when the companies were quite small.

A number of writers have begun to refer to this egalitarian style of management as the *clan* approach. This term is meant to imply that the organization is transformed to the point at which it becomes more like a very large extended family, with very close ties and relationships among all members of the "family" as contrasted with the typical impersonal bureaucratic organization. For example, Michael Beer (1985, p. 667) says:

Based on shared values, shared risks, and shared rewards, and oriented to a joint or collective achievement, the clan approach appeals to employees' desire to identify with and contribute to a social entity and to goals beyond immediate self-interest. For the clan approach to work there must be a gradual evolution within an organization of a shared set of beliefs that are regularly backed by supporting policy and action. An emphasis on this approach is associated with such consistently well-managed firms as IBM, Texas Instruments, and Kodak, as well as some of the outstanding Japanese firms.

Robert Levering, who coauthored *The 100 Best Companies to Work for in America* (1984, p. ix), defined the organizational characteristics of the 100 best companies in order to indicate what made these companies different. The first six characteristics described are:

1. Make people feel that they are part of a team or, in some cases, a family.
2. Encourage open communication, informing people of new developments and encouraging them to offer suggestions and complaints.
3. Promote from within; let employees bid for jobs before hiring outsiders.
4. Stress quality, enabling people to feel pride in the products or services they are providing.
5. Allow employees to share in the profits, through profit sharing or stock ownership, or both.
6. Reduce the distinctions of rank between top management and those in entry-level jobs; put everyone on a first-name basis; bar executive dining rooms and exclusive perks for high-level people.

One company that is legendary for creating a family environment is Delta Air Lines. Levering (1984, p. 74) talks about the corporate love affair between Delta employees and the airline:

A retiring Delta pilot took out a full-page ad in the *Atlanta Constitution* (at a cost of $8,000) to tell readers that "it has been my privilege to work with the finest group of human beings that God ever created" in "an organization that has been exceedingly well managed."

A few weeks later, three stewardesses announced that they and other Delta employees were pledging nearly $1,000 apiece to buy a $30 million Boeing 767 jet for the airline. "We just wanted to say thanks for the way Delta has treated us," one of the women explained. By December they had raised enough pledges to buy the 767. Seven thousand employees turned out at the Atlanta airport for the christening of "The Spirit of Delta."

Such expressions of affection may sound like the concoctions of a public relations flack. Not so. A large number of Delta employees genuinely love their company. They continually talk about "the Delta family feeling." Byron Carroll, a Delta mechanic for 18 years, told a reporter why he had contributed to the employee 767: "Delta's been good to me and my family. When my dad died, the company helped my wife and kids fly to the funeral, sent flowers, and several managers wrote letters. It meant a lot to me that they cared."

One of the payoffs for the company from Delta's family feeling is that it has been able to remain largely a nonunion company. It has, therefore, had much more freedom than other airlines to move employees to job slots where they were needed. And this flexibility is a primary basis for the company's profitability.

Like virtually all airlines, Delta has encountered financial difficulties, due in large part to deregulation. Its reaction, however, was fully in character with the family feeling. The *first* response was for the top executives to take a pay cut. A few months later other employees' salaries were frozen (but not cut). It is not hard to understand why employees love this company so much and why there is such a low turnover rate. You just don't resign from your family.

Another company that practices the clan style of management is Hewlett-Packard. The first thing that most people notice about Hewlett-Packard is the informal, friendly atmosphere. People obviously are relaxed and like each other. Everyone eats in the same cafeteria and no one wears a jacket. There is a great deal of laughter and conversation, both in the dining room and in clusters of employees throughout the company, at coffee break time and so on. But this friendly, relaxed, and egalitarian atmosphere is not a happy accident; it is carefully nurtured by numerous company policies and practices (Levering, 1984, p. 143):

- Free coffee and doughnuts are provided twice a day by the company, and there are informal beer busts in the afternoon.
- There are no time clocks and people can self-select their preferred eight-hour shifts.
- Work units are deliberately kept small.

- The office layout is a network of open partitions, with no doors on most offices.
- The company is famous for the practice of "management by walking around," which is intended to keep managers and executives in constant touch with other employees on an informal basis.
- The company once passed up an opportunity to buy another plant primarily because the plant had a plush air-conditioned executive suite, while the manufacturing area was not air conditioned.
- The company has a strict no-layoff policy.
- The company has developed a statement of its corporate philosophy called *The HP Way*, which includes the following items:
    Belief in people; freedom
    Respect and dignity; individual self-esteem
    Recognition; sense of achievement; participation
    Security; permanence; development of people
    Insurance; personal worry protection
    Shared beliefs and responsibility; help each other
    Management by objectives (rather than directives)
    Decentralization
    Informality; first names; open communication
- *All* employees participate in the same profit-sharing plan and are eligible for stock options.
- Separate executive performance bonuses are nonexistent.
- During a time of financial difficulty, *everybody* shared equally in a 10 percent across-the-board pay cut.
- The company encourages two-way communication not only by conducting surveys of employee attitudes, but also by publishing the results, management interpretations, and planned responses in the company magazine.

Putting people first and meeting the needs of employees is also considered a key competitive strategy at Federal Express. CEO Fred Smith says "We discovered a long time ago that customer satisfaction really begins with employee satisfaction. That belief is incorporated in our corporate philosophy statement—People, Service, Profit."

Johnson & Johnson actively pursues a family relationship with its employees. One practice that promotes this is decentralization. The company is divided into 150 different autonomous units in order to keep the work groups small. As a result, each employee can still have a feeling of working in a small company. Johnson & Johnson says in its *Credo:*[2]

We are responsible to our employees, the men and women who work with us throughout the world. Everyone must be considered as an individual. We must respect their dignity and recognize their merit. They must have a sense of security in their jobs. Compensation must be fair and adequate, and working conditions clean, orderly and safe. Employees must feel free to make suggestions and complaints. There must be equal opportunity for employment, development and advancement for those qualified. We must provide competent management, and their actions must be just and ethical.

Nissan, U.S.A, like Hewlett-Packard, goes to great lengths to achieve an egalitarian "family" relationship with its employees. Among the many policies and practices that support this culture are:

- *Any* Nissan employee with 12 months' service is eligible for the car-lease program (this is in sharp contrast to American auto companies, where only top executives are entitled to participate in the leasing programs).
- Nissan eschews virtually all executive perks because they are felt to run counter to Nissan's philosophy of "participative management."
- The employees are divided into small work groups or "teams," and the teams frequently meet on company time to discuss their work, plan modifications, and so forth.
- Everybody, including top executives, wears the company uniform, which has the Nissan logo (the company also supplies the uniforms).
- There is no executive dining room, and the president and other executives eat in the two large cafeterias with other workers.
- When in the plant, the president wears the same work uniform as the assembly-line workers, with his first name inscribed over the right pocket (all employees, incidentally, are on a first-name basis).
- The president conducts company-wide meetings of all employees at least quarterly.
- The company believes in cross-training, and each assembly-line worker is taught a variety of jobs.
- The day before a new employee reports for work, other employees call him or her on the telephone to provide a welcome to Nissan.
- Instead of basing pay on seniority, Nissan has a Pay-For-Skills Program, in which the employees' pay is determined by the number of different jobs that individuals can perform. The company provides training during working hours for those who wish to learn additional skills.

J.C. Penney Company reveres its close "family" relationship, and even goes to the extreme of encouraging relatives and multiple-generation families to work together. Penney's guiding philosophy is the Golden Rule ("Do unto others as you would have others do unto you"). All employees are called "associates" and are never referred to as employees. The store managers are called "partners." The company encourages employees at all organizational levels to socialize together, and it sponsors picnics to support this philosophy.

Although the connection may not immediately seem obvious, another management practice that can support an egalitarian clan culture is multiskilling and cross-utilization. In addition to developing the individual members of the workforce, multiskilling can also contribute to maintaining a stable workforce in turbulent times. This is because it is easier to retain people in difficult times if they have multiple skills. When Mazda suffered a severe decline in business, instead of laying off factory workers it put them to work selling cars. Besides retaining skilled workers and building the morale of the organization because of demonstrated commitment to supporting members of the organization "team," the company discovered, somewhat to its surprise, that the factory workers were among the top salespeople. After all, they could explain the product expertly and convincingly. Moreover, when production resumed its normal pace and they returned to the factory, an added bonus was that they had many useful ideas regarding customer reaction to the product.

The time has arrived in America for us to take a new look at some of the practices we take for granted. Of course, it may be decided that some status symbols, on balance, are contributing more to the organization than they are detracting from it, and these will need to be retained. But a careful, objective analysis may lead to the conclusion that many symbols have been around so long that we don't question them—and we should. It is time to begin such an analysis. Eliminating unnecessary barriers to communication lays the groundwork for increasing the involvement and participation of employees.

NOTES

1. Foulkes, Fred K. *Personnel policies in large non union companies.* Englewood Cliffs, NJ: Prentice-Hall, 1981.
2. Company document on the Johnson & Johnson website (http://www.johnson &johnson), 1997.

10 INVOLVING EMPLOYEES IN PLANNING AND IMPLEMENTING CHANGE: STEP 5 OF STRATEGY A

After executives have come to some preliminary conclusions about desirable organization changes, one very effective way of implementing participative management is to report to employees the actions already taken to change the organization, and then to invite the participation of everyone in the organization in planning further change.

In one company, the CEO announced, following a climate survey, "In last year's survey, over 70 percent of you asked for more information on company goals and objectives, so we are starting to distribute a monthly status report on corporate objectives and new business plans. Moreover, we are actively seeking the ideas of everyone in the organization for product improvements and new product applications." The excitement that resulted from this announcement bordered on pandemonium, and it was quickly apparent that the entire organization had been revitalized with new energy and commitment.

REPORTING RESULTS OF CHANGES ALREADY INITIATED

Exxon Corporation has set up a series of task forces to examine opportunities for improving productivity in each of a number of functional areas, one of which is human resources. The human resources force decided to use an opinion survey as a way to initiate productivity improvement programs. (Exxon managers have been using opinion surveys for many years, and they have a high level of expertise in applying survey techniques within their own company.)

The task force developed an opinion survey that included a number of questions dealing specifically with productivity improvement. They then asked for some departments to volunteer to participate in pilot studies. Surveys were undertaken within these departments and the results were fed back, in small meetings, to groups of employees who had participated. The employees were asked to interpret results and, by doing so, to identify issues or opportunities for improvement in productivity.

After this had been done, Exxon set up productivity task forces within each department, one for every specific productivity issue identified in the feedback sessions. The company is quite pleased with the results of this process.

IBM has adopted techniques very similar to those used by Exxon, including the development of some special productivity-oriented opinion surveys. As at Exxon, the responses are used as a basis for opening discussions by groups of employees to identify opportunities for improving productivity. IBM is also satisfied with the results of its efforts.

The managing director of a major New York consulting firm has said: "I find the efforts of Exxon, IBM, and other members of the Mayflower Group very exciting and encouraging; I believe we are on the verge of a substantial breakthrough that recognizes that the major opportunities for productivity improvement lie with people and are behavioral."

The experience of "Tidewater Bank" (a fictitious name, but a major corporation) illustrates how a climate survey can be used as an instrument for initiating organizational change in several geographically separate operating divisions of a company.

The president of Tidewater informed the bank's more than 1000 employees that, in order to measure how well the organization was doing in managing its employees, the bank had engaged a consultant to take a confidential climate survey. The survey was duly taken, the results analyzed by the consultant, and the results and conclusions communicated to the executives of the bank. The president of Tidewater felt that the data gathered had been quite helpful to management in assessing the overall condition of the bank's human resources. The president did find, however, that there were some major differences in the results from one division to another. He ultimately decided to embark on three courses of action in response to the survey data:

1. He began a series of meetings with key corporate executives and with key executives in each department to discuss the results, to identify some initial opportunities for improvement, and to plan a strategy for immediately beginning some of the changes decided upon.

2. He scheduled a series of open forum meetings throughout the bank to discuss the results of the survey, to announce the changes that had already been initiated in response to the survey data, and to solicit further suggestions from employees. He made it clear in these meetings that the bank was consciously moving toward a more participative culture and that both formal and informal systems were being installed to stimulate employee input.

3. He requested that each department in the bank form a *volunteer* task force committee to study the survey data for that department and for the bank as a whole. The departmental task force committees were asked to report back directly to the president (both in writing and in person at a meeting) their recommendations for organizational changes and improvements that should be implemented. The president emphasized that this was a completely open-end assignment, that no areas or issues were "off limits," and that while the climate survey data were to be the beginning point for discussion, the committees were not to feel limited to dealing with these data.

STIMULATING PARTICIPATION BY SEEKING FURTHER SUGGESTIONS

It is particularly helpful if top management can decide on at least a few very visible and significant changes to implement as a result of their initial review of the climate survey data. If at all possible, the changes should include some "sore spots" or nagging complaints that have been around the organization for many years. If management takes concrete action on some high-visibility, high-interest issues, this can serve as an important demonstration that the climate survey process is "real" instead of mere window dressing, and that it is going to significantly impact the organization. For example, if employees have complained for years about the poor condition of the parking lot, announcing some immediate action to correct the situation can have a very noticeable effect. If there have been widespread complaints about some aspect of the fringe benefit program, an announcement that, as a result of the climate survey, "the organization is committed to implementing specific changes in fringe benefits" can serve the same purpose. Even if it is not possible to provide a final decision on specific changes, a new sense of vitality can result from an announcement that a thorough study of some troublesome issue is about to be undertaken, and that top management is committed to some concrete action once the study has identified the best course.

Once the announcement of concrete changes resulting from the survey has set the framework and established the proper mood, the time is ripe to stimulate participative management. Ask employees for further suggestions for needed change. At the meeting where management's commitment to preliminary changes is announced, request that groups of employees take part in further discussions to interpret the survey data and generate specific suggestions for organizational improvement. Depending on the size of the group, this further analysis of data can involve all employees, or management can ask that rank-and-file employees elect representatives to serve on a task force. This committee can then act as liaison to the rank-and-file employees to obtain informal suggestions and ideas from them. These can be reviewed and discussed by the task force, along with consideration of the earlier survey data and the ideas generated by the task force itself, leading to a series of recommendations to top management. Maintaining a high level of communication and involvement is crucial to making this process effective; depending on the size of the organization, various kinds of communication devices will be very helpful in supporting this effort.

If the organization is small, informal communication may stimulate sufficient input to the task force. In most situations, however, it will be desirable to supplement this informal communication with one or more formal devices: employee newsletters, management memos, or regular articles in the company newspaper. All of these will report ideas and suggestions that have been put forward and will summarize the issues raised and discussed. In order to keep interest high, and the participatory change process motivated, any concrete results and specific changes implemented as a result of the previous work should be announced to employees frequently and emphatically.

It would be naive to suggest that all progressive efforts to stimulate participation will be successful, but it is also naive to suppose that organizations have reached the limit of constructive participation. While it is true that an overenthusiastic blind rush into bold participatory programs without prior study and analysis would in many cases be foolhardy, it is equally true that most organizations can no longer afford to be so conservative that they fail to explore the realistic opportunities for constructive participation.

The best way to assess the readiness of a particular organization for implementing increased participation is to analyze the data from a climate survey carefully, and to probe and explore the possibility of increased participation in discussing the results of the survey data with groups of rank-and-file employees.

In the typical organization there is widespread potential for constructive participation that has not yet been tapped. We can no longer afford to let this resource for improved organizational performance stand idle. The two most common complaints brought to light by climate surveys are:

1. People do not have as much information as they would like about the goals, objectives and future plans of the organization.
2. Employees do not have as much opportunity as they would like to suggest better ways of doing their own jobs and better ways of helping the organization to achieve its goals.

One company that has been notably successful in involving employees in interpreting the results of its annual employee attitude surveys and using teams of employees to generate suggestions for further organizational improvement is Federal Express. Each year, when the surveys have been tabulated, every manager receives the data both for her or his work group and for work groups throughout the company as well. The manager then calls a meeting of the work group and they review the results together. The group is expected to dig into the problems identified and come up with concrete proposals for improvement. This plan then goes into the manager's performance objectives for the next year, and the objectives are passed upward through the organization. This whole process is referred to at Federal Express as the survey-feedback-action program. Along with another program called "guaranteed fair treament," it is considered the backbone of the FedEx policy of using attention to employees as a major competitive strategy.

There is, in fact, a widespread desire on the part of employees throughout U.S. organizations to contribute their ideas and insight as well as their physical labor. The potential of this added contribution has been vividly demonstrated by organizations—such as Honda of America—that are achieving significantly better results (measured in terms of both productivity and quality) than their American competitors, even though their workforce is drawn from the same pool of workers.

We do, in fact, need the ideas, the full commitment, and the full contribution of all employees. The economy of the United States can no longer afford the luxury of settling for only half of the potential energy and contribution of its rank-and-file employees.

11 REMEASURING THE CONDITION OF THE HUMAN ORGANIZATION ANNUALLY: STEP 6 OF STRATEGY A

It can sometimes be helpful for an organization to use a climate survey even on a one-shot basis to identify opportunities for improvement and to initiate action. This is far from the best use of the tool, however, and it is not the thrust of Strategy A. Instead, Strategy A emphasizes the regular use of climate surveys as a routine management tool, either annually or every 18 months. Just as financial audits are done regularly, the audit of the human organization should also be done regularly. Like performance appraisals and compensation reviews, employee surveys can achieve their full potential for positive influence on the organization only when they become a continuing management tool.

One company that uses annual climate surveys as a routine management tool to identify opportunities for improvement and stimulate remedial action is IBM. It is very clear from the experience of IBM, Texas Instruments, Motorola, Hewlett-Packard and other firms that the value of climate surveys increases over time as they become accepted as additional sources of data for all kinds of management decisions.

USES OF THE EMPLOYEE SURVEY

One of the most important uses of the annual survey is the evaluation of previous managerial decisions, actions, and programs. The first survey will inevitably identify a number of opportunities for improvement. Top management will analyze these data carefully, discuss the data with others in management, and involve teams of employees from all ranks of the organization in discussing the data to generate suggestions for organizational change and improvement. Ultimately, management will decide on and implement a course of action—new policies, a revised management style, specific changes in training or compensation and benefits, an organization-wide development or change effort, and so on. Perhaps there will even be a decision to embark on a broad array of changes designed to move the organization toward a new corporate culture.

Once these changes have been implemented and their effect on the organization has become apparent, it is vital to evaluate whether or not that effect is the one that was desired. Has the human organization been strengthened, has it grown, has the planned-for improvement taken place, or has the organization merely moved sideways (or worse yet, declined)?

The best way to answer these questions is to remeasure the organization, using the same survey instrument previously employed. If there has been overall progress, this will be documented by a rise in the overall numerical index. If specific problem areas have been successfully addressed, this will be documented by a rise in the relevant factors of the index. Conversely, if there has been no progress and the planned changes have not occurred, this will also be documented. In either case, the results of the earlier managerial action provide needed evaluative data that can lead logically to the next cycle of management planning and action.

Depending on the results of the remeasurement, management may decide that the previous changes are indeed having the desired effect on the organization. This judgment will tend to reinforce the previous actions and will perhaps lead to a decision to continue the efforts already underway or even to expand them or broaden their application.

On the other hand, if the measurement shows that the previous actions are not "paying off" in the desired way, it will signal the need to rethink the problem and plan a new strategy. In either event, the remeasurement data provide a frame of reference for deciding on further action to be taken. Management of the human organization can be based on facts and data rather than on hunches or myths.

As with its function as a control mechanism to evaluate the effect of planned change, the climate survey also serves as an early warning system. In this regard it is like a quality control system that constantly samples and measures the product to alert those in charge quickly (that is, before too many defective products have moved off the line) when something goes wrong. Just as with a product quality system, knowledge that something is going wrong with the motivation or morale of the human organization alerts management to take corrective action *before too much damage has been done*. Of course, management will eventually find out about most problems even without a survey, but it may be several months before the trouble is evidenced by lower productivity and product quality, absenteeism, and employee turnover. By then, much damage may already have been done to the quality of the human organization (and to productivity), and it will take far longer to correct the situation. One of the great advantages of gathering regular climate survey data as a routine management tool is that it permits the *early* identification of trouble so that corrective action can be taken immediately.

As I have already pointed out, if we want executives to pay real attention (rather than just lip service) to the needs of employees as a primary strategy for achieving high levels of performance, it is essential that we both measure—and then pay for—the quality of their management of the human organization. The most accurate and objective measure of an executive's performance in managing the human organization is the score on an overall index and on the separate factors that make up a climate survey.

If an organization is serious about encouraging executives to use their human resources effectively, there is really no adequate substitute for an employee survey to measure this performance. Even if a regular climate survey were not needed to serve the planning and control functions already discussed, it would be necessary to implement one solely to tie executive compensation to effective utilization of the human organization. And unless we take the step to do this, the whole process of trying to change the organization's culture to emphasize attention to employee needs is just so much empty talk. Thus, another important plus of climate surveys is that they enable us to support many important organizational systems with a single management tool.

Creating a Continuous Hawthorne Effect

As discussed in Chapter 3, the term "Hawthorne Effect" refers to a phenomenon frequently observed by researchers. When research is being done with human subjects, the outcomes tend to be distorted by the favorable reaction of the human subjects to being participants in a study. The principle is that people enjoy the unusual attention paid to them by the researcher and react by wanting to change their behavior in the direction they think the researcher "wants" or expects.

While the "Hawthorne Effect" is quite an annoyance to researchers because it distorts their findings, it actually can work as a powerful tool for the manager whose primary interest is in influencing behavior in a positive direction for the organization. For such a pragmatist, positive results are far more important than scientifically accurate measurement.

Because people almost without exception appreciate the opportunity to express their feelings and ideas about the organization in a climate survey, the inevitable result, if the survey is properly conducted and appropriate action taken, is that the *measurement process itself* causes them to have a significantly more favorable attitude toward the organization. People often verbalize this direct connection in such terms as: "I really appreciate the company caring about my views, and I am sure this process is going to lead to constructive changes."

As a result, if a climate survey tool is used with skill and care, there is really a built-in bias that, over and above the effect of any changes initiated as a result of the survey, the process itself will tend to improve attitudes, motivation, and commitment. Although this effect is not automatic (it certainly is possible to misuse a survey in such a way as to cause harm), it is a commonplace observation by organizations using employee surveys over an extended period of time (for example, IBM, General Electric, Texas Instruments, Hewlett-Packard) that each time the organizational climate is measured, it tends to improve.

Thus, there appears to be an added bonus for the organization making routine use of employee surveys as a management tool—the process itself tends to initiate a self-fulfilling prophecy of improved organizational performance. It's as if people are giving the organization credit for just caring enough to make the effort.

This effect is particularly likely to result when management makes a regular practice of feeding the survey data back to employees at all levels, and teams of employees representing all functional areas are involved in analyzing and interpreting the data to generate recommendations for further improvement.

12 REINFORCING SUCCESS: STEP 7 OF STRATEGY A

It is very helpful to regularly analyze the correlation between climate survey data and hard criteria of organizational performance—productivity, profitability, growth, costs, and so forth. This information can then be used internally to reinforce the productivity improvement strategy when it is working effectively, and to point out the need for modification if the expected improvement in hard criteria has not been realized.

DETERMINING THE CORRELATION BETWEEN SURVEY DATA AND HARD CRITERIA OF ORGANIZATIONAL PERFORMANCE

Obtaining change in the organization culture and realizing improvements in organization climate, morale, and motivation are frequently not considered ends in themselves. These goals are thought of by most executives as means toward the longer-range objective of improved organizational performance. As William Ouchi points out in *Theory Z*, "Involved workers are the key to increased productivity."

Improvement in the end measures of productivity, profitability, growth, costs, and so on is the ultimate objective of most organizational change. We measure change in the intervening variable of climate, however, because change in performance takes longer to show up. We need interim indicators of how well our change strategy is operating, as milestones along the way.

Executives fully expect that change in the intervening measure of climate will accurately foretell later improvement in the ultimate criteria of organizational performance. For this reason, once a survey process has been in operation for several years, it is advantageous to make regular determinations of the correlation between changes in the measures of organization climate and changes in the measures of organization performance. This process can then serve as a control mechanism to assure that the organization change strategy is having the intended payoff in terms of profitability and other long-term hard measures of performance.

The simplest way to measure the relationship is to determine the linear coefficient of correlation over a series of years between the numerical data representing the organization climate and the numerical data representing the hard performance measures that have been selected. An example of this type of data is shown in Exhibit 12-1.

Because there will usually be a lag between improvement in organization climate and improvement in the end objectives of productivity and profitability, it is often helpful to determine the correlation between climate data in each particular year and the performance data one year later and two years later as well.

Using this approach, executives can visualize the impact that improvement in the condition of the human organization is having on the end measures that are the ultimate objective. This information

Exhibit 12-1 HRI *Scores and Operating Income*

Year	*HRI* Score	Operating Income ($Canadian)
1983		$36.3M
1984		36.4M
1985		47.8M
1986		45.8M
1987		35.6M
1988	3.08	40.7M
1989	3.18	52.5M
1990	3.18	45.8M
1991	3.19	55.0M
1992	3.23	66.9M

$r = 0.866$

enables the organization to evaluate the effectiveness of the change strategy and to respond appropriately.

REINFORCING SUCCESS

In the vast majority of cases where improvement in organization climate has been documented, the correlational analysis will show that there has been a corresponding improvement in the hard measures of performance (though frequently with a time lag of one to three years). The dissemination of this information throughout the organization can serve as a powerful reinforcement of the organization change process. Executives who lead the change process are reassured that it has produced some tangible bottom-line results. Their judgment and leadership are vindicated. Rank-and-file employees are reassured that their contribution of ideas, time, and commitment has been worthwhile for the organization. They are further reassured that the improved climate is likely to stay that way and the change process is likely to continue toward further improvements, since the process has had a rational payoff for the organization and its stockholders.

Perhaps most importantly, the positive data will serve to convince skeptical middle managers who may have resisted or taken a "wait and see" attitude toward the idea of improving attention to employees. It is hard to argue with positive bottom-line results, so all but the most reluctant will tend to be caught up by the spirit of an organization on the move and will feel social pressure to climb on board, rather than continuing to hold back.

The whole change process begins to develop a momentum of its own once positive bottom-line results have been demonstrated. This is the most important reason for this final step of Strategy A— reinforcing the strategy through determining and then publicizing the relationship between improvement in organization climate and improvement in organization performance.

Realistically, the ideas presented in this chapter may take four to six years to become fully operational in the typical organization. The process proposed here, while conceptually very straightforward, will be complex to implement in some organizations because of difficulty in collecting the performance data, and because of uncontrollable factors affecting performance measures. This does not mean, however, that we should delay beginning the measurement process.

What is proposed here, though technically complex, is doable and highly desirable as a long-term goal.

PLANNING MODIFICATIONS
WHERE NECESSARY

Of course, there is the possibility that analysis will show that improvement in climate has not been translated (even after a lag of two to three years) into improvement in the hard measures of organization performance. If this situation occurs, the data from the correlational analysis will alert top management of the need for further study to determine *why* no improvement in performance has been forthcoming and to plan for modification of the organization change strategy. The data literally provide the impetus as well as the rationale for initiating a trouble-shooting effort. If a cooperative, participative climate has been created, it will be appropriate and natural to enlist the widespread participation of employees at all levels in diagnosing *why* the improved climate has not led to improved performance. This process should lead to a strategy for redirecting organization effort toward the goal of improving the hard performance criteria. Once again, factual objective data about the condition of the human organization and its performance can become the best basis for involving *all* the talents and resources of the organization in planning improvement of that performance.

13 A FINAL WORD: DO IT NOW!

Work is a social as well as an economic activity—a fact long recognized by the Japanese, and the dominant philosophy of the Japanese approach to management. The roots of this philosophy also go deep into the history of management research and theory in America—the Hawthorne Studies in the 1930s and the work of McGregor, Likert, and Argyris in the 1950s and 1960s. And this philosophy has been the cornerstone of the management approach of some spectacularly successful organizations in America—IBM, Donnelly Mirrors (Donnelly Corporation), Hewlett-Packard, Delta Air Lines, Walt Disney, Federal Express, Southwest Airlines, and Motorola, to name a few. As Michael Mescon of Georgia State University says, "Showing people that you care is not being soft but being smart."

Given the perspective of this long and rich history, it is surprising that attention to employees has taken so long to become a dominant theme in American management thought. But now, finally, a revolution in management culture is underway in America. For at least the next decade, the dominant theme of American management practice will be the transformation of organizational culture toward more participative organizations that emphasize attention to employees as a major corporate strategy.

Strategy A is not a quick-fix approach to changing organization culture; it is a practical strategy for bringing about a fundamental change. Strategy A is designed to serve the needs of executives who desire to lead their organizations in a transition from a traditional bureaucratic culture to a participative, motivational culture emphasized by such organizations as IBM and Hewlett-Packard.

Strategy A emphasizes attention to the needs of employees as a key corporate strategy for achieving high productivity. It has been put forward as a practical seven-step approach for the organization or individual executive who wishes to launch a planned process of change to transform the culture of an organization. It is a rational, complete framework for such a transition, and provides practical guidance on where to begin and how to proceed.

The time has now arrived in many organizations to begin taking action. There are already far more data to support the utility of investing organizational energy in Strategy A than most organizations would demand before investing in new machinery, introducing a new product, or entering a whole new business.

Data from research with the *Fortune* 1300 largest companies (discussed in Chapter 2) have shown conclusively that a strategy of attention to employees pays off on the bottom line. Statistical analysis of the data from these leading companies has shown that those that emphasize attention to employees significantly outperform other companies in hard, measurable terms such as return on equity. Furthermore, detailed data from the many companies cited in this book illustrate exactly the process through which attention to employees is translated into superior financial performance. The way is now clear; what is needed is commitment to action.

THROWING OFF COMPLACENCY AND INERTIA

Comparing results from three surveys of the *Fortune* 1000 largest companies (conducted in 1987, 1990, and 1993) Lawler, Mohrman, and Ledford (1995) conclude that there is substantial evidence of a consistent trend toward increased adoption of employee involvement management practices, and that these have led to measurable improvements in financial performance. Nevertheless, they also conclude that adoption of employee involvement is still not widespread, and only a small minority of employees have opportunity for a high level of involvement. Although they predict continued evolution toward increased employee involvement, their data indicate that the traditional bureaucratic model of management still dominates the *Fortune* 1000. Seemingly, there is widespread recognition of the need to move toward high-involvement, employee-centered management, but companies are unsure how to move toward that goal.

In many organizations the hardest part of implementing Strategy A will be throwing off complacency and inertia, and dealing with resistance to change. In many organizations the status quo has been fairly comfortable *until recently*. Since competitive threat, either from abroad or at home, has been a fairly recent phenomenon for many organizations, executives have been lulled into a sense of complacency and are only now feeling real pressure to examine the organizational culture and management practices for opportunities to improve performance.

Another obstacle is resistance to change caused by reluctance on the part of management to give up special status, privileges, and perquisites. This very natural feeling was summed up best by an executive who said, "We have earned our status and privileges, why should we give them up?" It is to be hoped that enlightened self-interest will convince many executives of the desirability of voluntarily relinquishing status symbols and perquisites that retard organizational performance by raising barriers to cooperation and communication.

The change process will be further accelerated if executive pay is tied directly to performance of the *full range* of executive responsibility. In Chapter 8, I recommended a specific procedure for tying executive pay to *long-term* organizational performance using a balanced battery of objective performance indexes—including organizational climate data, turnover and absence statistics, and five-to-ten-year averages of financial performance. Where necessary, stockholders may choose to exert pressure (through the board of directors) on executives who are reluctant about tying executive reward practices more closely to the long-run interest of stockholders.

The most frequent cause of resistance to moving toward a more participative corporate culture, however, is the very sincere fear on the part of both executives and middle managers that they will lose power if the organization becomes more consultative and participative. This fear is based on the implicit assumption that there is a fixed amount of power and authority to go around in an organization. If employees gain more influence and power, so the thinking goes, someone else's power and influence must necessarily be reduced. If more attention is paid to the rank and file, if they are consulted and involved in decisions, then executives somehow must be diminished; they are the losers.

This is a shortsighted view that erroneously limits the definition of power to the concept of domination over others or over decisions. If we expand the definition of power to include the ability to accomplish objectives, it is much easier to see that, by sharing information, influence, and decision-making authority in the organization, the individual executive's power to achieve high performance goals may be greatly enhanced. This is the secret discovered by Thomas Watson at IBM, John Donnelly at Donnelly Mirrors (Donnelly Corporation), Sidney Harman at Harman International, and Dave Packard at Hewlett-Packard. This is the guiding philosophy not only of these organizations but also of Delta Air Lines, McDonald's, Sufco, and Motorola.

What these organizations have discovered is that power is *not* a fixed quantity that has to be divided up in a zero-sum game. Power can be expanded so that everyone can gain it simultaneously. What one group or individual gains does not have to be lost by others. The total amount of power available to all in the organization can be expanded greatly once we think of it as *power through others* to achieve results rather than as *power over others* to dominate in making unilateral decisions.

One of the reasons that power expansion through participative management and attention to employees has worked so well where it has been tried in the United States is that this management style is true to the American ideal of democracy and egalitarian treatment. The democratic, participative style of management fits our culture so much better than an autocratic, authoritarian style of management that violates fundamental American values. It is Theory Y that is consistent with American cultural values. Theory X is really the aberration, even though it became the dominant management style in America.

This is why it so ironic that the participative, employee-centered style of management, which sprang originally from American values and culture, and which was pioneered by American management writers and entrepreneurs, was first widely adopted and popularized in Japan. To ask whether these management practices can be adapted to American organizations is absurd; they are far more at home here than in Japan. It was the Japanese who had the problem of cultural adaptation. To their great credit, however, the Japanese have performed an important service by demonstrating convincingly that these values and management practices work particularly well with American workers in such organizations as Nissan of

America (in Tennessee), Sony (in California), Quasar (in Illinois), and YKK Zipper (in Georgia).

THE PAYOFF IN FUN AND EXCITEMENT

There is a significant added benefit for organizations that are ready to make a commitment to Strategy A. That benefit is the payoff in added fun and excitement as well as financial performance. Although this book has stressed the financial payoff that results from attention to employees, it is equally true that Strategy A organizations are simply more exciting, more fun, and more interesting for their members at every level. That's one of the main reasons Nissan of America has not only higher productivity and quality than General Motors, Ford, or Chrysler, but better labor relations as well. Workers at Nissan have lower absenteeism, higher productivity, and higher morale at least in part because they have more interesting jobs. They are treated as valued associates rather than hired hands, so they think of themselves as part of the "team" or "family." Instead of criticizing top management's high salaries and bonuses (as workers have at the American Big Three automakers) their attention is focused on improving productivity so *all can share* in the results.

It is also clear from the comments of all ranks of employees (including executives) at Hewlett-Packard, Donnelly Mirrors (Donnelly Corporation), and IBM that they enjoy their jobs, and they like their organizations and the others they work with. Their jobs are an important and meaningful part of their lives, rather than drudgery merely to earn a living. This is a side benefit enjoyed by executives no less than by rank-and-file workers. When Harman International published information on the organization's culture and management style, they were deluged with resumes from executives and professionals who wanted to sign on with the company. This will increasingly be the reaction of younger, highly educated executives who want an open, cooperative, supportive environment in which to work rather than the repressive hierarchical organizations of the past.

PRODUCTIVE ORGANIZATIONS CAN AFFORD TO BE HUMANE

Happily for all, highly productive organizations can afford to be more humane. This is really the essence of McGregor's Theory Y.

The most effective (that is, productive) way to manage is to create an organization culture in which each individual perceives that it is possible to achieve his or her own *personal* goals *best* by cooperating with others to achieve the goals of the organization. Similarly, it is possible to fully achieve the goals of the organization over the long run only by making it possible for individuals to achieve *their* goals in the process.

Such a culture is not a utopian dream. This book has discussed several organizations that are competing in real markets using this management strategy with great success. For the organization wishing to embark on the transition to such a culture, Strategy A stands ready to help. It is no longer reasonable to say, "I would like to move my organization toward a culture that emphasizes attention to employees as a strategy for achieving high performance, but I don't know where or how to begin." The way to proceed is to start with Step 1 of Strategy A and then follow the process through to Step 7. This process is referred to as Strategy A because it is based on the experience and practice of the most effective and financially successful firms in America. To reinforce their importance, the Seven Steps are repeated in the next section.

STRATEGY A: SEVEN STEPS TO HIGHER PRODUCTIVITY THROUGH EFFECTIVE USE OF THE HUMAN ORGANIZATION

1. Determine the baseline condition of the human organization through measurement, using a validated and standardized employee survey instrument. Although executives often believe that they have an accurate feel for the morale of the organization, this is rarely the case. Interestingly, they seem to underestimate the level of satisfaction and morale about as often as they overestimate.

2. Based on the survey data, identify and act on key opportunities for improvement—cost effective "winners" worthy of special attention because of a high payout/investment ratio. Some likely candidates are:

   • Improve communication, especially regarding organization goals and objectives.

   • Increase participation of rank-and-file employees in important management decisions.

- Rationalize the *distribution* of rewards by really linking pay and other rewards directly to performance, since numerous studies show that pay is by far the most powerful motivator of improved work performance.
- Implement a flexible compensation program that allows each employee to custom-tailor the mix of compensation and fringe benefit options to match personal preferences and obligations. This approach enables the company to obtain 100 percent motivational value for every dollar spent on compensation and benefits.
- Consider adopting a productivity bonus plan that allows employees to share tangibly and directly in the improved financial results of *their* successful efforts to increase productivity. There is a very simple principle involved in this suggestion: If you want people to increase productivity, pay them for it.

3. Change executive evaluation and reward practices to measure and pay for effective human resource management as well as the traditional measures of profit, productivity, and cost. If we really want executives to take the long-term perspective of building the human organization, we have to measure this performance and include it in pay determination. We must move toward measuring performance by long-term results instead of year to year, and we need to commit our organizations to sacrifice short-term profits for long-term control of markets.

4. Remove artificial barriers to participation, communication, and contribution. Among the barriers that an organization might consider for elimination are such divisive symbols as separate dining rooms, reserved parking spaces, elaborate differences in office space and furnishings that exceed actual work requirements, and other unnecessary marks of status. In many organizations, careful evaluation of these practices may lead to the conclusion that they are anachronisms, appropriate perhaps to another era, that have now outlived their usefulness.

5. Report to employees what has been done to change human resource management assumptions and practices, and solicit their participation in planning further change. This is a way of directly implementing participative management.

6. Measure again the condition of the human organization using the same standardized survey instrument to determine changes.

Repeat this standardized measurement of human resources annually, and:

- Use this measure as an evaluation tool for managers.
- Feed data back to employees at all levels of the organization. Involve teams of employees representing all functional areas in analyzing and interpreting the data to generate recommendations for further improvement. Although review teams may be advisory only, top management should commit to giving their views a great deal of weight.

7. Measure the correlation between the employee survey data and hard criteria of organizational performance—productivity, profitability, growth, costs, and so forth. Use this information to reinforce the productivity improvement strategy and to modify it if necessary.

To reiterate, on the basis of accumulating evidence, it appears that increased attention to employees is going to have a major impact on organizations during the next decade. Companies that begin to manage their human resources effectively to harness the untapped potential for commitment to the goals of the organization will forge ahead, while others will find they are unable to remain competitive.

APPENDIX: MANAGEMENT PRACTICE, ORGANIZATION CLIMATE, AND PERFORMANCE— AN EXPLORATORY STUDY

Frederick E. Schuster, Professor of Management
    Florida Atlantic University
D. Larry Morden, Senior Vice President
    Ault Foods, Ltd.
Thomas E. Baker, Managing Partner
Ian S. McKay, Managing Partner
    People Interactions Inc.
Karen E. Dunning, Director, Strategy & Business Planning
    Motorola, Inc.
Christine M. Hagan, Doctoral Candidate
    Florida Atlantic University

We thank Benjamin King for his advice and invaluable assistance regarding the data analysis.

This study reports a single time series quasi-experiment in a Canadian firm to evaluate the effect over a five-year period of implementing a structured seven-step strategy to obtain improved organization performance through employee-centered management.

A significant change in the condition of the human organization resulting from the intervention was measured over the five-year period and shown to be correlated with a 66 percent increase in profitability.

The results of the study indicate that in the Canadian/U.S. context, employee-centered management is at least compatible with high performance and competitive advantage. There is also evidence that in some instances organization performance can be significantly enhanced through the participation and contribution of employees in problem-solving and decision-making processes.

The relationship among management practice, organization climate, and performance has been of considerable interest to researchers and to the business community for some time. Much of the early discussion of this relationship was based on conjecture and informal case studies. In the last few years, there has been an increase in formal, empirical studies attempting to identify and describe the linkages among these concepts. Understanding the nature and direction of the relationships, and how the underlying energies can be harnessed, focused, and controlled, has important implications for productivity and business results.

An earlier study (Schuster, 1986) of the 1000 largest industrial and 300 largest nonindustrial firms in the United States found a significant relationship between employee-centered management and financial performance. In this study, "employee-centered management" was defined as a strategy for achieving high levels of employee motivation, commitment, and performance through management practices (such as participation and involvement) that emphasize attention to employee needs and goals. Other studies (Blackburn and Rosen, 1993; Lawler, 1986, 1992) have strongly supported the role of employee involvement in achieving improved organizational performance. Huselid (1994) has recently reported similar results in a parallel study. Employee involvement has been defined by Lawler (1986, 1992) as consisting of four critical organizational processes: information sharing, training, decision making, and rewards. According to Lawler, employee involvement refers to the degree to which these four key processes are moved down to the lowest levels in the organization.

Lawler contends that the key to organizational effectiveness lies in completely changing the way organizations are managed. In order to be competitive, organizations will require highly skilled, knowledgeable workers and a relatively stable workforce. Traditional hierarchies must be transformed into organizations in which individuals know more, do more, and contribute more. This high-involvement or

employee-centered management model is based on the belief that people can be trusted to make important decisions about the management of their work. This approach puts knowledge, power, rewards, and a communications network in place at every level in an organization. It encourages employees to know how to do their work, to care about the work they do, and to do it as well as it can possibly be done. It is important to note, according to Lawler (1992), that the real basis for competitive advantage lies in the management systems that create and sustain this environment. He cautions us not to confuse effective management systems with high-quality employees:

This is a mistake—the two are quite different. . . . Having high-quality employees does not assure an organization of having sustainable competitive advantage or even a short-term advantage. If the employees are poorly motivated or if the correct organization systems are not in place, the employees' talent may be wasted.

According to Lawler, an organization becomes employee-centered through a carefully managed process that strives for participation to integrate the individual with the organization to achieve high productivity and competitive advantage. This process involves restructuring the work so that it is as challenging, interesting, and motivating as possible. Individuals at all levels are given power to influence decisions; they are given information about the organization's operations and performance; they are trained so that they can operate with a good understanding of the business.

If the smoothly-running assembly line is the best image for the control-oriented approach, then the small business unit that controls its own fate and involves everyone in the business is the best image for the involvement-oriented approach.

Only in the past few years have empirical studies begun to quantitatively measure organization climate and its relationship to organization performance. Hansen and Wernerfelt (1989) used the Survey of Organizations in 60 publicly traded firms to measure two organizational factors: (a) emphasis on the management of human resources, and (b) emphasis on goal accomplishment. Examining variation in rates of profitability, they determined that these organizational factors were "significant determinants of firm performance . . . ," and that they explained about twice as much variance as economic factors.

·Dennis Kravetz (1988) noted that some organizations have made deliberate changes in management style and workplace philosophy, reflecting a commitment to emphasize the human side of business. Questioning whether such management practices (which he termed "progressive") were associated with bottom-line results, he studied human resource management and philosophy across nine dimensions of 150 large companies and compared these measures to financial performance. The results:

nearly every financial criterion examined showed a strong relation to human resources progressiveness. The more progressive companies had much better financial results than the less progressive firms. The results were significant not only from a statistical standpoint but from a practical standpoint as well. The magnitude of group differences in sales growth, profit margins and other criteria has a tremendous impact on each company's success. If less progressive firms could attain the financial results of the highly progressive companies, not only would individual companies be better off, but the national economy would improve greatly as well.

The central proposition that emerges from the studies reviewed here is that conscious interventions to move an organization toward emphasizing high levels of employee involvement and enhanced emphasis on meeting employee needs can produce higher motivation and commitment, leading to improved organizational performance. Although this is by no means a novel idea in the management literature, the previous evidence for this proposition has been largely anecdotal. This study is designed to test empirically the proposition that an intervention strategy to produce enhanced employee involvement and attention to the needs of employees can produce significant improvement in hard financial measures of organizational performance.

One measurement issue that has been the subject of lively debate in the recent management literature is the question of whether linearly aggregated individual employee perceptions constitute an appropriate measure of *organizational* climate. This study explicitly adopts the macro-culture view of James, Joyce, and Slocum (1988), who argue that personal frames of reference are the only legitimate measures of culture/climate—at the individual level and then aggregated to represent groups and organizations. It also reflects the views of Hofstede, et al. (1990), who extensively utilize statistical analysis to conclude that it is both acceptable and reasonable to use aggregated individual data to represent a group for comparison with other groups or across time.

As a result of the mounting research evidence cited here and the positive experience of pathfinder firms, more and more companies in the United States are turning to employee-centered management to enhance productivity and quality, and to gain the competitive advantage of a workforce fully committed to the organization's goals. Organizations are increasingly recognizing that efforts to improve productivity and quality must include attention to the human organization—its motivation, commitment, and morale. For example, a major component of the scoring system for the Malcolm Baldrige Award involves accounting for the state of the organization's human resources.

Increased attention is therefore being paid to developing tools for analysis and strategic management of the human organization. These tools may be used for measuring its condition, evaluating its performance, and initiating corrective action when needed to bring performance in line with organizational objectives. A number of leading firms have pioneered the development of survey systems that facilitate such measurement.

METHOD

The Research Design

The study utilized a single time series quasi-experimental design to measure the effect of a seven-step intervention strategy on the dependent variable of operating income. This is a powerful design for inferring the effect of such an intervention over time on a dependent variable (Campbell and Stanley, 1963; Cook and Campbell, 1979; Judd and Kenny, 1981).

The Survey Instrument

The survey instrument used in this intervention to implement employee-centered management was the *Human Resources Index (HRI)* (Schuster, 1986). The *HRI* is a standardized employee survey instrument that measures 15 key dimensions of employee perceptions regarding the work environment. The *HRI* contains 64 positive statements about the organization, for which each employee is asked to indicate her or his level of agreement using a five-point scale. The 64 items are scored and reported individually; they are

also used to determine a composite score on each of the following 15 dimensions or factors:

1. Reward system
2. Communication
3. Organization effectiveness
4. Concern for people
5. Organizational objectives
6. Cooperation
7. Intrinsic satisfaction
8. Structure
9. Relationships
10. Climate
11. Participation
12. Work group
13. Intergroup competence
14. First-level supervision
15. Quality of management

A composite *HRI* score, computed by weighting equally each of the 64 individual items, represents the summary evaluation by employees of conditions within the organization at a particular point in time. This overall *HRI* score is the initial basis for analyzing and comparing results from one organization with another, or in comparing changes over time within a single organization. The composite *HRI* score is the best single measure of change over time in the overall condition of the human organization because, as would be expected, the composite *HRI* score has higher reliability than any of the separate factors.

The reliability of the overall instrument and of the individual factors was determined using Cronbach's Alpha, a statistic widely accepted as a general purpose measure of reliability. The alpha coefficients calculated for the total instrument and for the individual factors are shown in Table A-1. The reliabilities ranging from 0.757 to 0.929 were judged to be more than satisfactory to justify further use of the instrument.

The validity of the instrument was determined through a process of content validation.

The Subject Firm

The subject firm for this study is a diversified dairy products processing and marketing firm of about 3000 employees widely dispersed in several major regions of Canada. It is recognized as one of

Table A-1 *Coefficient Alpha Reliabilities*

Scale	Alpha Coefficient
Total Instrument	0.978
Factors:	
Reward system	0.774
Communication	0.894
Organization effectiveness	0.901
Concern for people	0.828
Organizational objectives	0.874
Cooperation	0.852
Intrinsic satisfaction	0.888
Structure	0.757
Relationships	0.765
Climate	0.929
Participation	0.852
Work group	0.766
Intergroup competence	0.799
Quality of management	0.866

the leading dairy processors and distributors in North America, with annual sales in excess of $1.4 billion.

Data collection has been ongoing since 1988; annual measures of organization climate representing all employees (using the *Human Resources Index*) now exist for five data points. The data have been collected with breakdowns by division, plant or department, function, level, and gender.

The Intervention

A corporate strategy was initiated at the subject firm in 1987 to develop and sustain competitive advantage in order to better compete in the global marketplace. A key element in that strategy was the recognition by executive management that sustainable competitive advantage could be achieved only through the participation and contribution of all employees. The new participative management system introduced into the organization was intended to:

* Involve all employees to ensure maximum input and impact on five critical business success factors (quality, customer service, cost effectiveness, innovation, and managing the environment)

- Change the way in which the business is managed by making every employee an individual manager of his or her job
- Establish an environment that encourages employees to express ideas freely and resolve workplace problems quickly and fairly
- Utilize the input of employees who are closest to issues in their identification and resolution
- Empower employees through sharing of decision-making authority

Each employee is a member of a work team in the participative management system, sharing a common vision and reporting relationship. Membership in work teams is compulsory, although participation levels differ depending on the interest of individual members. Team leaders are the first-line supervisors, but this role quickly evolves into a facilitator/coaching relationship.

The work team system provides the opportunity for team members to provide input into the problem-solving and decision-making processes. Work teams interact on an *ad hoc* basis with members of other work teams when mutual issues occur or when the services and/or products delivered by one group significantly impact the performance of the other work team.

The other component of the empowerment technology at the subject firm is the fairness/equity system, in which each work team elects a representative to the location Equity Committee. The role of the committee is to monitor the effectiveness of the management system, resolve issues of fairness/equity in treatment of employees after their failure to come to a satisfactory decision with their immediate supervisors, and to provide recommendations on new or modified policies. Each location Equity Committee selects a representative to participate as a member of the Corporate Equity Committee, which meets to address unresolved fairness/equity issues submitted by one of the location Equity Committees and/or new or modified policy recommendations. All decisions made at any level of the fairness/equity system must be by consensus. No issues that are covered by the terms and conditions of a Collective Bargaining Agreement fall within the purview of the equity committees.

A key element in implementing employee-centered management has been use of the *Human Resources Index (HRI)* to track progress of the change process. The integration of the *HRI* into corporate management strategy reflected top management's conviction that employee-centered management could create the ultimate sustainable competitive advantage. The *HRI* has provided benchmarks on key performance indicators, measurement of the effectiveness of human resource interventions, identification of improvement opportunities, and the process to involve employees in improving organizational performance. This process is consistent with the principles of the new employee-centered management system, which is seen as a key strategy for developing and sustaining competitive advantage.

Strategy for Implementing Employee-centered Management

The strategy employed for implementing employee-centered management consists of the following seven steps:

1. Determine the baseline condition of the human organization using a validated and standardized survey instrument. Many executives believe that they can sense whether the morale of the organization is high or low, but this is seldom the case. In a recent study of a large bank, for example, the chief executive officer (CEO) was elated to discover that the teller group had a much higher level of morale and commitment to the organization than he had believed. On the other hand, he was appalled to discover that the top officers were among the most dissatisfied.

2. Use the survey data to identify and act on key opportunities for improvement worthy of special attention because of a high payout/investment ratio. Although the opportunities that will surface will be unique to each organization, some candidates that will arise in many organizations are:
   a. Improve communication, especially where organization goals and objectives are concerned.
   b. Increase participation of rank-and-file employees in important management decisions.
   c. Rationalize the distribution of rewards by linking pay and other rewards directly to individual or group performance.
   d. Implement a flexible compensation program that allows each employee to choose compensation and fringe benefits on the basis of personal preferences and obligations.
   e. Consider adopting a productivity bonus plan that allows employees to share tangibly and directly in the improved financial results from their successful efforts to increase productivity.

3. Change executive evaluation and reward practices to measure and pay for effective management of people as well as profit, productivity, and reduced costs. If executives are to build the human organization over the long term, this performance must be measured and included in pay determination.

4. Remove artificial barriers to participation, communication, and contribution. Such barriers include separate dining rooms, reserved parking spaces, elaborate office space and furnishings that exceed actual work requirements, and other unnecessary status symbols. Careful evaluation of these practices may indicate that they are anachronisms, appropriate perhaps to another era, that have now outlived their usefulness.

5. Report to employees what has been done to change management assumptions and practices, and solicit their participation in planning further change. This is one way of directly implementing employee involvement.

6. Measure again the condition of the human organization using the same standardized survey instrument to determine changes. Repeat this standardized measurement annually, and:
   a. Use this measure as an evaluation tool for managers.
   b. Feed data back to employees at all levels of the organization. Involve teams of employees representing all functional areas in analyzing and interpreting the data to generate recommendations for further improvement. This is another means for directly implementing employee involvement.

7. Measure the correlation between the *HRI* data and hard criteria of organization performance—productivity, profitability, growth, costs. Use this information to reinforce the performance improvement strategy and to modify it if necessary.

The Intervention Process

In addition to overall corporate results at the subject firm, the *HRI* scores are broken down each year by specific location, organizational level, job function, gender, and divisional groupings.

Both top management and the human resources management staff at the firm frequently express the judgment that the most powerful element of the intervention to implement employee-centered management has been the process each year of feeding numerical results and written commentary back to teams of employees in each location for review, analysis, and recommendations. The following four-step process is used:

Step 1. A review committee of nonmanagement staff is formed and meets to receive the pertinent information on the *HRI* (including background on its development, the scoring methodology, and the identification of statistically significant differences), copies or summaries of the written commentary (depending on the preference of the review committee), and location *HRI* results by question and factor. This step in the process is usually completed within two hours.

Step 2. The review committee identifies and prioritizes the issues arising from the *HRI* review, denotes specific concerns for each of the issues, and develops proposed action plans for their resolution. This step is usually completed within 12 to 16 hours and requires a follow-up meeting to review and modify the written proposal to be presented to the management committee.

Step 3. The review committee presents its issues, specific concerns, and proposed corrective action plans to the management committee. The management committee frequently requests points of clarification or amplification. This presentation usually lasts 2 to 3 hours.

Step 4. Usually within a six-week period, the management committee prepares and presents a written response to each proposed action plan—indicating a commitment to proceed, a modification to the proposed corrective action plans with reasoning, or a rejection of the proposed corrective action plan with justification. All approved recommendations or modifications include designated accountability and targeted dates for completion.

Quarterly follow-ups with the review committees by the management committee are conducted to communicate and discuss progress on the corrective action plans.

Management committee feedback on the process confirms that the issues and priorities established by review committees parallel the thinking of management. The management committee has also commented that the employee-developed corrective action plans confirm management's perspectives on the results of the *HRI*, sometimes permit management to act on plans it had rejected because management incorrectly perceived that employees would be opposed, or sometimes bring to light plans never considered by management.

The review committees generally have been very satisfied with this four-step review process because it provides the opportunity for employees to identify and understand the issues in the workplace that negatively impact productivity and profitability, and improves relationships within the employee group as they meet colleagues from each department/function and listen to differences in perspective on the issues and their resolution. Management is viewed as taking the time necessary to review their proposals and put in writing their commitment to action plans; the process confirms that management is serious in requesting employee input.

Use of the Survey Data

The following are specific examples of how the survey data have been used to plan and evaluate initiatives to improve organizational effectiveness:

1. At the beginning of the organization change process in 1987, the research and development group was targeted as a pilot group for involving a whole function in a planned change effort. Innovation in technology and processing had been identified as a key pillar of the organization's strategic thrust toward improved competitiveness; thus, it was felt that the research and development group had a critical role to play in driving technological improvements throughout the company. However, the group was experiencing difficulties in working together. The employee group would not even meet in the same room with their managers; trust was nonexistent. The *HRI* data were used within the research and development group to focus attention on employee involvement and to deal with issues of concern to employees. In the first survey year the overall *HRI* score for the R&D group was 3.35. A number of issues were identified by employees as problem areas: the weak link between pay and performance, an unsatisfactory compensation program, management's lack of concern for people, absence of a supportive climate, and limited opportunity for participation in decision making. Following a number of changes implemented over the next year regarding rewards, communication, management style, and participation, the overall *HRI* score increased to 3.79, a statistically significant change. Moreover, it was widely recognized that the work climate had changed significantly. The survey item concerning a supportive and trusting climate increased from 2.86 to 3.86, a statistically significant change. Today the R&D group is consistently viewed as one of the firm's top performing groups; it has developed many product and process

innovations that are key to the organization's financial progress. Moreover, the R&D group continues to use the *HRI* data each year to continuously evaluate and improve its own operations and performance.

2. The flagship operation introduced the new employee-centered management system during 1990–1991. On item 48 of the *HRI,* which states "People can participate in and influence decisions which are important to the operation of their work unit," the 1992 results increased to 3.19 from the 1991 results of 2.98. This statistically significant difference confirms that the new management system has been recognized by the employees at this location as contributing to their participation in the problem-solving and decision-making processes. The effectiveness of the new management system at this flagship operation is critical because of its key role in the success of the organization.

3. In response to employee suggestions, a corporate-wide improvement to the pension plan was initiated and communicated shortly after the *HRI* was completed in 1991. Item 22 of the Index states "The pay and fringe benefits are attractive," and the results for this item increased in 1992 to 3.59 from the 1991 score of 3.45. This statistically significant increase indicates that employees perceived their overall compensation to be positively affected by this improvement in the pension plan, since salary increases were average in comparison to the marketplace in 1991 and no other improvements were made to the benefit package.

4. In response to organization-wide *HRI* survey data, a corporate environmental committee was established in 1990 and mandated to develop an integrated environmental policy and implementation plan, with specific focus on waste management systems, recycling, and reuse of packaging materials. The communication of plans by this committee occurred in 1991. On item 36 of the *HRI,* which states "This is a socially responsible organization in every way (its products, waste disposal, marketing techniques, employment practices, etc.)," the results in 1992 for the total organization increased to 4.16 from the 1991 results of 3.83 (a statistically significant improvement), indicating a positive impact on employee perceptions of the organization's social responsibility.

5. At a location that had implemented the new employee-centered management system in 1989, results for item 19 of the *HRI,* which reads "Goals and objectives are established with the

involvement of those who are to achieve the goals," *decreased* from the 1991 score of 3.27 to the 1992 score of 2.94. Based on the results of the *HRI,* a review committee (including representatives from all levels and functions within the operation) was formed to investigate the ineffectiveness of the new management system, determine the specific problems that required attention, and develop a proposal for corrective action. The review committee recommended replacement of the general manager at that location because his management style was viewed as inconsistent with the values of employee-centered management. With replacement of this manager, the results on the same *HRI* item rose to 3.29 the following year. An overall F test was performed on these data; the results are shown in Table A-2. Pairwise F tests were also performed to compare the 1991 data with the 1992 data, and the 1992 data with the 1993 data; the results of the pairwise comparisons are shown in Table A-3. All of the F values are significant at the 0.01 level.

6. At the corporate office, the results for item 45 of the *HRI,* which reads "My superior knows and understands the problems of his/her subordinates," *decreased* from a score in 1991 of 3.61 to a score of 3.00 in 1992 for the administrative support staff. A review committee of administrative support staff met to discuss the results for this question and determined it was caused in part by the introduction of electronic and voice mail technologies, which reduced the need for regular boss/subordinate communication meetings. A recommendation was made to senior management that regular meetings be reestablished. This recommendation was accepted and implemented; in the next survey, the response on the same item rose to a level above the initial level of 3.61.

Additional insight into how the *HRI* is being used to implement and monitor organization change can perhaps best be provided with an excerpt from the summary report of a recent administration of the *HRI*:

Perhaps the most significant finding is that 12 locations have shown a steadily upward trend over the period 1988–1993. For the total organization it is particularly gratifying that the individual factors which have shown the most improvement are Participation and Communication—both factors which are directly the focus of employee-centered management. Moreover, of equal importance is the fact that *each* of the 15 factors shows an increase over the period 1988–1993, and also from last year to this year.

Table A-2 *Overall Analysis of Variance—1991, 1992, 1993*

	Mean	N	Var.	Std. Dev.	SS	df	MS	F
1991	3.27	123	1.050	1.025				
1992	2.94	175	1.008	1.004				
1993	3.29	225	1.063	1.031				
Between					13.97	2	6.98	6.718*
Within					540.51	520	1.04	

* $p < 0.01$

Table A-3 *Pairwise Analysis of Variance—1991, 1992 and 1992, 1993*

	Mean	N	Var.	Std. Dev.	SS	df	MS	F
1991	3.27	123	1.050	1.025				
1992	2.94	175	1.008	1.004				
Between					7.90	1	7.90	7.684*
Within					304.46	296	1.03	
1992	2.94	175	1.008	1.004				
1993	3.29	225	1.063	1.031				
Between					12.34	1	12.34	11.905*
Within					412.37	398	1.04	

* $p < 0.01$

RESULTS

The results obtained over a five-year period by the subject firm following the intervention to implement employee-centered management are shown in Table A-4 and Exhibit A-1.

The top executives of the organization selected a single audited financial figure, "operating income before non-recurring expenses," as the most valid and relevant criterion to evaluate the effect of the intervention. They selected this single criterion for three reasons:

1. It was felt to reflect directly internal operations and be less contaminated than other measures by external economic factors unrelated to the intervention,
2. It was an audited financial figure already used internally as the primary gauge of performance; therefore,
3. It could be readily understood and accepted as a valid measure of progress by all members of the organization.

Table A-4 HRI *Scores and Operating Income*

Year	*HRI* Score	Operating Income ($Canadian)
1983		$36.3M
1984		36.4M
1985		47.8M
1986		45.8M
1987		35.6M
1988	3.08	40.7M
1989	3.18	52.5M
1990	3.18	45.8M
1991	3.19	55.0M
1992	3.23	66.9M

r = 0.866

Exhibit A-1 *Time Series Plot*

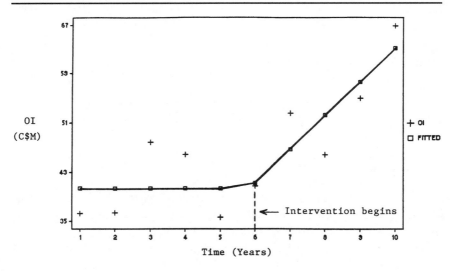

Exhibit A-1 shows the trend line reflecting financial performance of the firm (operating income before nonrecurring expenses) over the five-year period 1983–1987, which immediately preceded the intervention to implement employee-centered management, and over the five-year period 1988–1992 following the intervention. To test the significance of the change in the slope after the intervention, a 0 to 1 intervention indicator and an interaction term were created as shown in Table A-5. Then, a linear model was fitted to the two independent variables. Originally we included Time in the regression equation, allowing for estimation of a nonzero slope before the intervention. The regression coefficient for Time, however, had a very high p-value; therefore Time was dropped from the model. The equation for the predicted values is

$$OI = b_0 + b_1\text{Intervention} + b_2(\text{Time} \times \text{Int})$$

where Intervention = 0 if Time $\leq$ 5; 1 if Time > 5. The statistical package used was Statistix for Windows from Analytical Software, Inc.

Exhibit A-1 shows that the trend of operating income has shifted upward following the implementation of employee-centered management. Operating income of $66.9 million in 1992 represents a 66 percent increase over the average operating income of $40.38 million for the five-year period that preceded the intervention.

Table A-5 *Unweighted Least Squares Linear Regression of Operating Income*

Time	Operating Income (OI) ($ Canadian)	Intervention	Time × Intervention
1	36.3M	0	0
2	36.4	0	0
3	47.8	0	0
4	45.8	0	0
5	35.6	0	0
6	40.7	1	6
7	52.5	1	7
8	45.8	1	8
9	55.0	1	9
10	66.9	1	10

Predictor Variables	Coefficient	Std. Error	Student's t	p
Constant	40.3800	2.59447	15.56	0.0000
Intervention	−32.1200	15.12820	−2.12	0.0714
Time × Int	5.4900	1.83457	2.99	0.0202

r-Squared	Adjusted r-Squared	MSE	Std. Dev. of Residual
0.7338	0.6578	33.6564	5.80142

Source	DF	SS	MS	F	p
Regression	2	649.501	324.7510	9.65	.0097
Residual	7	235.595	33.6564		
Total	9	885.096			

| Cases Included | 10 | Missing Cases | 0 | | |

The usual diagnostic tests were applied to the residuals, and there was no evidence of autocorrelation or violation of other regression assumptions. A more sophisticated model such as ARIMA was not feasible because of the small number of observations. The time series regression analysis performed is sufficient to confirm that the effect of the intervention is substantial, and the difference in slope before and after the intervention is significant at the 0.02 level, as shown in Table A-5.

For seven degrees of freedom, the 0.05 value of t (2-tail) is 2.365; therefore, the 95 percent confidence interval for the pre- and post-intervention difference in slope is $5.490 \pm (1.83457 \times 2.365)$. Thus, the 95 percent confidence interval ranges from 1.1512 to 9.8288. Although the confidence interval is wide, it does not include zero; therefore, again, the intervention effect is confirmed.

HRI Scores and Financial Performance

The correlation between yearly *HRI* scores and financial performance over the period 1988–1992 is 0.866, as indicated in Table A-4. By squaring the correlation coefficient between *HRI* scores and operating income (r = 0.866) we obtain the coefficient of determination, which is 0.75. This statistic tells us that change in the condition of the human organization accounts for or explains 75 percent of the variation in financial performance (operating income).

DISCUSSION

While it is impossible to prove causality with absolute certainty, the data strongly support the conclusion that improvement in the motivation, morale, and commitment of the human organization in the subject firm has led to significantly improved organizational performance, rather than vice versa. Certainly this is the widely held conviction of individuals throughout all echelons of the organization, from top management to the level of operating employees.

The *HRI* scores were typically obtained early in each year, and the financial results for that fiscal year were not determined until several months later. This time sequence of events would seem to make backward causality (that improved performance leads to improved attitudes) unlikely in this particular situation. Also, while it is true that the trend of all 15 factors has been upward over the six-year period, the two factors that have improved the *most* are Participation and Communication, the two factors that are most directly the focus of the intervention to implement employee-centered management. The increase of both of these factors is statistically significant, as is the increase of the overall *HRI*.

Further, although this is subjective evidence, the fact is that people throughout the organization, at all levels and in all functional areas (including the union leadership), simply attribute the significant improvement in financial performance to the improvement in morale and commitment within the organization, rather than the other way around.

Further perspective for interpreting the improvement in performance of the subject firm over the five-year period is provided by comparing its performance with the performance of its major competitors. Over the time period 1988–1992 the subject firm significantly outperformed *each* of its competitors in the Canadian industry. The performance of the entire industry in Canada was essentially flat over the time period 1988–1992, while the subject firm was experiencing its 66 percent increase in operating income.

With the exception of the subject firm and one other firm, these are nonpublic companies and therefore financial data are not published. Financial information is shared internally within the industry by the companies through their industry association, which supplied the evaluation of comparative performance for this research study. The subject firm was also recognized by *Dairy Foods*, the dairy industry association journal, as Dairy Processor of the Year for 1992 *because of their outstanding financial performance relative to the industry as a whole.*

The superior performance of the subject firm cannot be accounted for by any unique environmental, economic, or competitive factors that affected the firm differentially as compared to the balance of the industry; the only difference was the change in internal management practices relative to the implementation of employee-centered management. Specifically, the authors attempted to carefully investigate whether there might have been significant changes in economic, demographic, or product market conditions that affected the firm differentially; or whether company location differences, government regulations, access to markets, or any other differences or changes in the external environment might have somehow favored the subject firm. Despite careful study of these matters, it was not possible to discover any external environmental factors that might have accounted for even a small portion of the performance improvement.

Moreover, there were no significant internal changes within the organization over the five-year period other than those directly related to the intervention to introduce employee-centered management. There were no significant organization restructurings, changes in employment level, or changes in business strategy (such as product design, product niche, marketing, or process technology), independent of the intervention, that might account for the improved performance.

As part of the employee-centered management intervention, however, there was a substantial investment of organizational resources (financial and human) to train both managerial and nonmanagerial personnel in the skills and behaviors required for employee-centered management. Driven by the intervention strategy described above, a number of other organizational changes were made in response to employee feedback and the recommendations of review committees—for example, widespread changes toward a participative management style and employee involvement in decision making, breaking down of barriers and significant improvement in communication, improvements in the pension plan, and the environmental initiative described earlier. Favorable reaction to these changes no doubt contributed both to the significant improvement in *HRI* scores and to the significant improvement in financial performance reported. However, from the perspective of the researcher, the executive management committee, and the several employee review committees it would be erroneous, to speak of these changes as *independent* causes of the improvements reported. The changes were, in fact, part of the initial design of the intervention strategy. One could even speculate about bidirectional causality (that is, although improved financial performance is initiated by the organizational change effort, once it is reported the improved financial performance may then cause further improvement in attitudes). Such speculation misses the point that, if these effects exist, they are part of the intervention and not an *independent* causal variable. Simply stated, although the authors searched carefully for external environmental conditions or *independent* strategic changes that might serve as alternative explanations, the only plausible interpretation seems to be that the improvement in organizational performance is a direct consequence of employee-centered management and employee-recommended changes resulting from the intervention.

As a result of its significant improvement in performance, the firm has become widely acknowledged as an industry leader in Canada. As previously stated, in recognition of its performance breakthrough, it was designated by the dairy processing industry as Dairy Processing Firm of the Year for all of North America in 1992.

IMPLICATIONS AND CONCLUSIONS

Certainly one clear implication of these findings is that interventions to implement employee-centered management have the potential to create significant improvement in organization performance.

The experience of the Canadian dairy products company illustrates that, for some organizations, significantly improved organization performance can be achieved through the participation and contribution of employees in problem-solving and decision-making processes.

Participative approaches will not, however, fit the circumstances of all organizations. Because the active, wholehearted support of top management seems to be essential to the successful implementation of employee-centered management, the approach described should not be implemented unless top management is truly convinced that it represents the *best* opportunity to achieve sustainable competitive advantage.

Nevertheless, in the competitive 1990s, when many organizations are seeking to achieve significant breakthroughs in operating performance, the seven-step strategy described here for implementing employee-centered management will likely fit the needs and circumstances of a wide range of organizations and therefore warrants serious consideration. The probability of "fit" with a wide range of organization should be boosted by the fact that the seven-step strategy described is a *contingent* strategy that builds in adaptation to differing organizational conditions.

Of course, the real test of the robustness of this strategy for implementing employee-centered management will be replication in a wide variety of circumstances. The authors are currently involved in conducting this study in very divergent organizations. Necessarily, however, the results of such longitudinal studies cannot be available for several years. One objective, therefore, of publishing the findings of this exploratory study is to encourage replication by others, so that it will be possible to investigate the effect of this strategy in a wide range of organizations simultaneously.

REFERENCES

Blackburn, R., and Rosen, B. 1993. Total quality and human resources management: Lessons learned from Baldrige award winning companies. *Academy of Management Executive,* 7(3): 49–66.

Campbell, D. T., and Stanley, J. C. 1963. *Experimental and quasi-experimental designs for research.* Chicago: Rand McNally & Company.

Cook, T. D., and Campbell, D. T. 1979. *Quasi-experimentation: design & analysis issues for field settings.* Chicago: Rand McNally College Publishing Company.

Hanson, G. S., and Wernerfelt, B. 1989. Determinants of firm performance: The relative importance of economic and organizational factors. *Strategic Management Journal,* 10: 399–411.

Hofstede, G., Neuijen, B., Ohayv, D., and Sanders, G. 1990. Measuring organizational cultures: A qualitative and quantitative study across twenty cases. *Administrative Science Quarterly,* 35: 286–316.

Huselid, M. A. 1994. Documenting hr's effect on company performance. *HR Magazine,* 39(1): 79–85.

James, L. R., Joyce, W. F., and Slocum, J. W. 1988. Comment: Organizations do not cognize. *Academy of Management Review,* 13(1): 129–132.

Judd, C. M., and Kenny, D. A. 1981. *Estimating the effects of social interventions.* Cambridge: Cambridge University Press.

Kotter, J. P., and Heskett, J. L. 1992. *Corporate culture and performance.* New York: Free Press.

Kravetz, D. J. 1988. *The human resources revolution: Implementing progressive management practices for bottom-line success.* San Francisco: Jossey Bass.

Lawler, E. E. III. 1986. *High involvement management: Participative strategies for improving organizational performance.* San Francisco: Jossey Bass.

Lawler, E. E. III. 1992. *The ultimate advantage: Creating the high involvement organization.* San Francisco: Jossey Bass.

Lawler, E. E. III. 1994. Total quality management and employee involvement: Are they compatible? *Academy of Management Executive,* 8(1): 68–76.

Pfeffer, Jeffrey. 1994. *Competitive advantage through people.* Boston: Harvard Business School Press.

Schuster, F. E. 1986. *The Schuster report: The proven connection between people and profits.* New York: John Wiley & Sons.

SELECT BIBLIOGRAPHY

Akin, G., and Hopelain, D. 1986. Finding the culture of productivity. *Organizational Dynamics*, 7(2): 19–32.

Argyris, Chris. 1957. *Personality and organization*. New York: Harper & Row.

Barney, J. B. 1986. Organizational culture: Can it be a source of sustained competitive advantage? *Academy of Management Review*, 11: 656–665.

Beer, Michael, et al. 1985. *Human Resource Management: A General Manager's Perspective*. New York: Free Press.

Beer, Michael, and Spector, Bert. 1985. *Readings in human resource management*. New York: Free Press.

Beer, Michael, Spector, Bert, Lawrence, Paul R., Mills, D. Quinn, and Walton, Richard E. 1985. *Human resource management: A general manager's perspective*. New York: Free Press.

Bettinger, R. 1989. Use corporate culture to trigger high performance. *Journal of Business Strategy*, 2: 38–42.

Blackburn, R., and Rosen, B. 1993. Total quality and human resources management: Lessons learned from Baldrige award winning companies. *Academy of Management Executive*, 7(3): 49–66.

Brewster, C. 1995. Towards a "European" model of human resource management. *Journal of International Business Studies*, 26(1): 1–21.

Cameron, K. 1986. A study of organizational effectiveness and its predictors. *Management Science*, 32(1): 87–112.

Carroll, D. 1983. A disappointing search for excellence. *Harvard Business Review*, 6: 78–88.

Cascio, W. F. 1982. *Costing human resources: The financial impact of behavior in organizations*. Boston: Kent-Wadsworth.

D'Aprix, Roger. 1982. The oldest (and best) way to communicate with employees. *Harvard Business Review* (September–October).

Denison, D. R. 1984. Bringing corporate culture to the bottom line, *Organizational Dynamics*, 13(2): 5–22.

Denison, D. R. 1990. *Corporate culture and organizational effectiveness*. New York: John Wiley & Sons.

Drucker, Peter F. 1973. *Management: Tasks, Responsibilities, Practices.* New York: Harper & Row.

Ewing, David W., and Banks, Pamela. 1977. Participative management at work, an interview with John F. Donnelly. *Harvard Business Review* (January–February).

Faux, Victor A. 1973. *Donnelly Mirrors, Inc.* Boston: Harvard Case Clearing House.

Fingleton, E. 1995. *Blindside: Why Japan is still on track to overtake the U.S. by the year 2000*. Boston: Houghton Mifflin.

Gordon, G. G. 1985. The relationship of corporate culture to industry sector and corporate performance. In Kilman, Saxton, & Serpa (Eds), *Gaining control of the corporate culture*, 103–125. San Francisco: Jossey Bass.

Gordon, G. G., and DiTomaso, N. 1992. Predicting corporate performance from organizational culture. *Journal of Management Studies*, 29(6): 783–798.

Hanson, G. S., and Wernerfelt, B. 1989. Determinants of firm performance: The relative importance of economic and organizational factors. *Strategic Management Journal*, 10: 399–411.

Hofstede, G., Neuijen, B., Ohayv, D., and Sanders, G. 1990. Measuring organizational cultures: A qualitative and quantitative study across twenty cases. *Administrative Science Quarterly*, 35: 286–316.

Homans, George C. 1941. *Fatigue of workers*. New York: Reinhold.

Hunter, J. E., Schmidt, F. L., and Jackson, G. B. 1982. *Meta-analysis: Cumulating research findings across studies*. Beverly Hills: Sage.

Huselid, M. A. 1994. Documenting hr's effect on company performance. *HR Magazine*, 39(1): 79–85.

Huselid, M. A. 1995. The impact of human resources management practices on turnover, productivity, and corporate financial performance. *Academy of Management Journal*, 38(3): 635–672.

IBM Corporation. 1974. *Manager's guide to the opinion survey*. Armonk, NY: IBM Corporation Publication.

James, L. R., Joyce, W. F., and Slocum, J. W. 1988. Comment: Organizations do not cognize. *Academy of Management Review*, 13(1): 129–132.

Karatsu, Hajime. 1984. The "japan bashers" are wrong. *Pacific Basin Quarterly*, 11: Winter/Spring.

Kinney, Harrison. 1982. As you see it. *THINK, the IBM Magazine*. Armonk, NY: IBM Corporation (November/December).

Kochan, Thomas A., and Barocci, Thomas A. 1985. *Human resource management and industrial relations*. Boston: Little, Brown.

Kopelman, R. E., Reinharth, L., and Beer A. A. 1983. The link between judgmental rewards and performance. *Personnel Administrator* (April).

Kotter, J. P., and Heskett, J. L. 1992. *Corporate culture and performance*. New York: Free Press.

Kravetz, D. J. 1988. *The human resources revolution: Implementing progressive management practices for bottom-line success*. San Francisco: Jossey Bass.

Lawler, E. E. III. 1986. *High involvement management: Participative strategies for improving organizational performance*. San Francisco: Jossey Bass.

Lawler, E. E. III. 1992. *The ultimate advantage: Creating the high involvement organization*. San Francisco: Jossey Bass.

Lawler, E. E. III. 1994. Total quality management and employee involvement: Are they compatible? *Academy of Management Executive*, 8(1): 68–76.

Lawler, E. E. III, Mohrman, S. A., and Ledford, G. E. Jr. 1995. *Creating high performance organizations*. San Francisco: Jossey Bass.

Lawrence, P., and Lorsch, J. 1967. *Organization and environment*. Boston: Harvard Business School Press.

Levering, Robert, et al. 1984. *The 100 best companies to work for in America*. Reading, MA: Addison-Wesley.

Likert, Rensis. 1961. *New patterns of management*. New York: McGraw-Hill.

Loomis C. J. 1982. The madness of executive compensation. *Fortune* (July 12)

Management. 1978. A productive way to vent employee gripes. *Business Week*, (October 16).

McGregor, Douglas. 1960. *The human side of enterprise*. New York: McGraw-Hill.

Moffett, Matt. 1984. Great productivity at a Utah coal mine is called "god's plan." *Wall Street Journal*, (April 12).

Naisbitt, John. 1982. *Megatrends: Ten new directions transforming our lives*. New York: Warner.

Nollen, S. D. 1979. Does flextime improve productivity? *Harvard Business Review*, (September/October).

Ouchi, William G. 1981. *Theory z: How american business can meet the Japanese challenge*. Reading, MA: Addison-Wesley.

Peters, T. J., and Waterman, R. H. 1982. *In search of excellence*. New York: Harper & Row.

Petitpas, Georges. 1980. Productivity—and what the personnel executive can do about it. (A presentation to the Nashville, Tennessee, Chapter of the American Society for Personnel Administration.)

Pfeffer, J. 1994. *Competitive advantage through people*. Boston: Harvard Business School Press.

Posner, B., Kouzes, J., and Schmidt, W. 1985. Shared values make a difference. *Human Resources Management*, 24: 293–309.

Reynolds, P. D. 1986. Organizational culture as related to industry position and performance: A preliminary report, *Journal of Management Studies*, 23: 333–345.

Saffold, G. W. III. 1988. Culture traits, strength and organizational performance: Moving beyond "strong culture." *Academy of Management Review*, 3(4): 546–558.

Schein, E. H. 1994. *Organizational culture and leadership*. 2nd ed. Lake Forest, IL: Brace-Park Press.

Schmidt, F. L., Hunter, J. E., and Pearlman, K. 1982. Assessing the economic impact of personnel programs on workforce productivity. *Personnel Psychology*, 35: 333–347.

Schuster, F. E. 1979. *Harman International Industries, Inc*. Boston: Intercollegiate Case Clearing House.

Schuster, F. E. 1982. The human resources index: A tool for evaluating and controlling the management of human resources. *The Personnel Administrator* (October).

Schuster, F. E. 1985. *Human resource management: Concepts, cases, and readings*, 2nd ed. Reston, VA: Reston.

Schuster, F. E. 1986. *The Schuster report: The proven connection between people and profits*. New York: John Wiley & Sons.

Schuster, F. E. 1995. *Contemporary issues in human resource management*. New York: McGraw-Hill.

Schuster, F. E., and Dunning, K. E. 1982. *Survey of human resource management (hrm) practice*. Boca Raton, FL: Administrative Systems Research Center, Florida Atlantic University.

Sease, Douglas R. 1985. Japanese firms set up more factories in U.S., alarm some americans. *Wall Street Journal* (March 29).

Shaiken, H. 1988. High tech goes third world. *Technology Review*, 38–47.

Simmons, John, and Mares, William. 1982. *Working together—employee participation in action*. New York: New York University Press.

Skinner, B. F. 1989. *Recent issues in the analysis of behavior*. Columbus, OH: Merrill Publishing Co.

Skinner, W. 1981. Big hat. *Harvard Business Review*, 5: 106–114.

Special Report. 1981. A new way of managing people. *Business Week*, (May 11).

Staff of the United States General Accounting Office. 1981. *Productivity-sharing programs: Can they contribute to productivity improvement?*

Washington: United States General Accounting Office.

Steers, Richard, and Porter, Lyman. 1983. *Motivation and work behavior.* New York: McGraw-Hill.

Tsurumi, Yoshi. 1984. The big lies of the Japanese conspiracy theory— deja vu the Nazis' Jewish conspiracy theory. *Pacific Basin Quarterly,* 11: Winter/Spring.

Tsurumi, Yoshi. 1984. The Japanese conspiracy: A new hoax on the American public. *Pacific Basin Quarterly,* 11: Winter/Spring.

Vroom, Victor. 1995. *Work and motivation.* San Francisco: Jossey-Bass.

Wagner, J. A. III. 1994. Participation's effects on performance and satisfaction: A reconsideration of research evidence. *Academy of Management Review,* 19(2): 312–330.

Wallace, M., and Fay, C. 1983. *Compensation: Theory and Practice.* Boston: Kent-Wadsworth.

Waterman, R. 1994. *What America does right: Learning from companies that put people first.* New York: W.W. Norton.

Wilkinson, A. L., and Ouchi, W. G. 1983. Efficient cultures: Exploring the relationship between culture and organization performance. *Administrative Science Quarterly,* 28: 470–476.

INDEX